TALKING
SKETCHING
MOVING

TALKING
SKETCHING
MOVING

Multiple Literacies in the Teaching of Writing

PATRICIA A. DUNN

Boynton/Cook
HEINEMANN
Portsmouth, NH

Boynton/Cook Publishers, Inc.
A subsidiary of Reed Elsevier Inc.
361 Hanover Street
Portsmouth, NH 03801–3912
www.boyntoncook.com

Offices and agents throughout the world

Library of Congress Cataloging-in-Publication Data
Dunn, Patricia A., 1952–
  Talking, sketching, moving : multiple literacies in the teaching
of writing / Patricia A. Dunn.
    p. cm.
  Includes bibliographical references and index.
  ISBN 0-86709-570-9
  1. English language—Rhetoric—Study and teaching. 2. Report writing—Study
and teaching (Higher) 3. Multiple intelligences. 4. Critical pedagogy. I. Title.

PE1404 .D86 2001
808'.042'0711—dc21

                                                                    2001035605

Editor: Lisa Luedeke
Production service: Denise Botelho, Colophon
Production coordinator: Elizabeth Valway
Cover design: Jenny Jensen Greenleaf, Greenleaf Illustration & Design
Manufacturing: Steve Bernier

Printed in the United States of America on acid-free paper
05 04 03 02 01 DA 1 2 3 4 5

To my mother and father,
Rita B. Dunn and Joseph B. Dunn

I would like to thank all students who were willing to try thinking in different ways and for allowing me to use their work in this book.

I am also grateful to Illinois State University for a research grant that partially funded this work.

And special thanks to Ken Lindblom for his encouragement and support.

Contents

Foreword

As I explained to Patricia Dunn during our discussions regarding this foreword, I had two very strong responses to the book you have before you. On the one hand, I was simply impressed: delighted by its readability; struck by the range of material it draws upon and marshals to such good effect; and, most notably, entranced by its narrator, who manages to be gracious, generous, even self-deprecating, but also pointed, passionate, and critical in the best of academic senses. A bit of this part of my reaction, no doubt, can be attributed to the self-indulgent pride of a former teacher—I was lucky enough to work with the author when she was a doctoral student—but the book would warrant it in any case. It is a good read, a terrific performance.

On the other hand—and precisely because it was so effectively written—the book made me squirm. I had no trouble understanding that its narrator was pointedly, passionately critical of the way I am inclined to teach writing—or, more precisely, of the way I am inclined to teach writing to people whose favored modes of learning are not the same as my own. Midway through the second chapter, Patricia offers a sketch of the kind of people who end up teaching writing, and poses for them some hard questions:

> Composition specialists today were most likely yesterday's linguistically talented students moving up in a linguisto-centric school system that privileged our way of knowing. But what if schools used only math or only drawing or only dance as a way of knowing? How would our word-loving brains have reacted? Would we have had the success in school and the confidence in ourselves that we needed to seek higher degrees?—to pour our energies into this language-loving discipline?

Talk about hitting home. Certainly I was one version of that student, and indeed I am always ready to point to all sorts of quasi-analytical explanations about why: extended bouts of illness as a child that promoted lots of reading time; my mother, who was an inveterate reader; and encouragement from an extended family (so that when my same-age cousins got toy shotguns one Christmas at the big family gathering, I got a set of paperback classics). In any case, and for whatever reasons, written language was my thing, and school was indeed the place where it paid off in the most durably reinforcing ways. I was good at school insofar as school rewarded certain kinds of writing—certain kinds of text-making performance, as I've come to think of them—and I pursued such performances insofar as I liked being good at school.

On those grounds alone, then, I fit Patricia's profile. Perhaps more to the point, however, I am acutely aware of the extent to which time and occupation and inclination have conspired to make the teacher I have become even more the linguisto-phile (if that is the right play on linguisto-centric)—even more the "English dork," as my children say—than I ever was as a student. So, for example, I have had any number of days in the past twenty-five years—certainly hundreds, maybe thousands of them—during which I spent more of my waking hours alone and writing than among people, interacting . . . and was really happy about it. Or, to take a somewhat different emblem, I am far more comfortable right this moment, at this keyboard, than I will be later today at lunch with a job candidate, say, or in my classroom, or at the faculty meeting. In short, to a degree that I could never have imagined back when I was my version of that linguistically talented student, textual space has become home to me: it defines not only what I do, but also, and in a very profound sense, it defines who I am, and does so in ways that very directly affect my teaching.

All of which is by way of saying that for someone like me, at any rate, a book called *Talking, Sketching, Moving: Multiple Literacies in the Teaching of Writing* constitutes a much-needed wake-up call, a stern reminder that the world of print-based prose I experience as so familiar, natural, and comfortable absolutely will not seem so warmly hospitable to most of my students. Indeed, in ways and for reasons that this book is at some pains to document, a good many of them will experience that world as remote, alien, and threatening. Written language will not have been their thing as it was mine. Rather, as the book's title suggests, their aptitudes and inclinations, their ways of learning and knowing and being in the world, will take other forms, and would be better represented in their talking, sketching, moving, and so on. If I am to help them learn to write, therefore—and not, say, confirm for them (again, probably) that my world of print-based writing simply isn't their kind of place—then I need to devise a pedagogy that not only recognizes those inclinations and aptitudes, but seeks to harness them. And this book is an excellent point of departure for both of those destinations, Chapters 1 and 2 on the former, Chapters 3 through 6 on the latter.

Nothing about the alterations Patricia Dunn proposes will be easy. When I declared that the book makes me squirm, I meant it. I don't like to be told that I am preserving my comfort in the classroom at my students' expense—especially when the case presented is so convincing. I like it even less when I am shown how to remedy that situation, because it means . . . well, because it means giving up my comfort, and I have surely earned that, no? "Well," my onetime student in essence replies herein, "no, you haven't, and you don't really want it. Teachers need to continue developing too, always, not only because it is a duty, but because learning with and from our students is where the joy lies. So come on, old man, get ready to talk, and sketch, and move." And of course—don't you hate it when this happens?—she is absolutely right.

Stephen M. North
University at Albany,
State University of New York

Introduction

Multiple Literacies

In this book, I argue that we take better advantage of multiple literacies, that we investigate and use whatever intellectual pathways we can to help writers generate, organize, reconceptualize, and revise thoughts and texts. The metacognitive distance all writers need—on a draft, on an idea, on their thinking—can come through visual, aural, spatial, emotional, kinesthetic, or social ways of knowing, or unique combinations of them. I also argue that we should have greater expectations for all our students, resisting the urge to use one way of making knowledge—writing—as a gauge of their intellectual capabilities. Those who for whatever reason are not "good writers" should be expected to call upon other strengths to enhance the linguistic-based tasks English Studies requires. Those already "good writers" should be expected to develop what may be for them lesser-used representational systems (talking, sketching, moving, etc.) as ways to gain deeper insights on their print-based work. All writers would benefit from multiple intellectual pathways to generate knowledge, and the world in general would benefit from the intellectual contributions of people traditionally excluded by print-loving pedagogies.

In the early chapters, I point out how univocal Composition theory has become in promoting the importance of language, especially writing, in knowing, so much so that these beliefs may be affecting our openness to other theories of knowing. I argue further that Composition has taken some of its most influential theorists and lopped off for its use only *part* of the theory espoused by them. There were and are a number of people who embrace ways of knowing beyond writing and language, but their language-as-knowing statements are the ones repeatedly selected in Composition citings of their work. What *else* they endorse regarding the role speech, visualization, and movement play in learning has been consciously or unconsciously de-selected.

Within our field, ideas related to multiple ways of knowing have surfaced in the theories and practices of some of our most influential teacher/scholars. James Moffett depended heavily on drama as a way for writers to obtain intellectual distance on ideas. Nancy Martin, who with James Britton did much to launch the language-based reform movement in London that was the forerunner to the Writing Across the Curriculum movement in the United States, did much work with play. Lev Vygotsky called play, which included the physical action involved in it, "a leading factor in development" (1978, 101), but Vygotsky is mostly cited in our field to support theories on the importance of the social in learning. Even Janet Emig, whose essay "Writing as a Mode of Learning" David Russell credits with heavily influencing the field's shift to a focus on *writing* as a unique mode of learning, supported writing over speech partly because speech could not then be easily transcribed. And Paulo Freire, who was deeply interested in how people come to know, used what today would be called multiple intelligences in his teaching. As we shall see in Chapter 2, few who cite Freire foreground that important aspect of his praxis.

That people make knowledge in ways other than writing is an idea that has been posited and demonstrated in disciplines beyond Composition and Rhetoric. Thomas West has written about mathematicians and scientists visualizing theories before writing them down. Allan Gross, Susan Eriksson, and others have pointed out that Charles Darwin's theory of evolution was a sketch called "A Tree of Life" before it was described in words.[1] Darwin's sketch was an intricate drawing, a huge tree with different-sized branches connecting to a central trunk. According to Gross (1999) and Eriksson (1999), Darwin used this sketch and metaphor to conceptualize and work out his theory. Only then did he write it down.

Howard Gardner (1995) has focused attention on seven and then eight "multiple intelligences": linguistic, logical-mathematical, spatial, bodily kinesthetic, musical, interpersonal, and intrapersonal. The eighth is "naturalist intelligence," a way of discerning patterns in the natural world.[2] Daniel Goleman (1995) has foregrounded the importance of "emotional intelligence," and Antonio Damasio (1999) has shown the role emotions play in thinking. These insights from other fields, however, have not impacted writing theory and practice in substantial ways.

Whether the idea of alternate ways of knowing comes from outside or inside Composition, however, it is an idea that, with too few exceptions, has been ignored or dismissed. I will end by arguing for a critical synthesizing of divergent theories of learning. These theories may appear at times contradictory in an either/or loving culture. However, we should take advantage of any perceived contradictions—or "contraries," as Peter Elbow would call them—for the productive dialectic they provide for keeping us always questioning what we're doing and why.

In "Modernism and the Scene(s) of Writing," Linda Brodkey wants to disrupt a cliché about writing: the scene of a writer working alone in a garret, isolated from social forces. Instead, she wants to shift our conception of writing to encompass "the very social, historical and political circumstances from which garrets have been defending us" (1987, 413). She says, "To see writing anew, to look at it from yet other vantage points, we must re-read an image that we have come to think of as the reality of writing. It is not enough to say that it is only a picture, for such pictures provide us with a vocabulary for thinking about and explaining writing to ourselves and to one another" (399). Similarly, I would like to disrupt clichés, commonplaces, and romanticized scenes of writing held by pundits in the media as well as by theorists in Composition. I want to disrupt remaining myths about literacy: that "smart" people write well; that "dumb" people don't; that writing is itself the best heuristic for carrying out the intellectual work involved in writing; and that oral, visual, or kinesthetic approaches to generating, organizing, or revising texts are acceptable for "basic" writers but not "serious" intellectual pathways for "real" writers.[3]

I am not the first person inside or outside Composition to make a case for using "multiple channels of communication" (Paulo Freire's phrase) to supplement the teaching of writing and textual study. As I will explain more thoroughly in Chapters 1 and 2, a number of people in Composition or related fields have made similar arguments: Linda Hecker, Karen Klein, Peter Smagorinsky, Joan Mullin, Pam Childers, Eric Hobson, Dan Kirby, Tom Liner, and Ruth Vinz. Rita Dunn and Kenneth Dunn have done extensive work in the secondary schools with their model of 21 "elements" or learning styles, which are influenced by environmental, emotional, sociological, and physical factors (1993, 3–4).[4] With too few exceptions, however, we in Composition have not taken up either the theories informing this work or practices that would result from it because of our limited assumptions about how people come to know, as well as a vested interest in promoting language-based epistemologies. We should expect more of ourselves and our students.

Throughout the chapters, I use a number of different phrasings to describe the various ways people come to know and the approaches we might use to take advantage of those ways. Sometimes I borrow Howard Gardner's phrase "multiple intelligences," and sometimes Mary Belenky and colleagues' "ways of knowing." I like Brenda Bruggemann's use of "alternative formats" for teaching diverse populations, and Donna LeCourt's recommendation for using "multiple literacies" in Writing Across the Curriculum reform. I also use the phrases "multisensory approaches," "alternate strategies," "diverse intellectual pathways," and others. I especially admire Paulo Freire's phrase "multiple channels of communication" because he was aware of their importance over forty years ago, seeing their link with student confidence, thinking, and knowing. I use these phrases interchangeably and realize that other users may take issue with that decision. I deliberately intermix these terms to avoid being locked into one epistemological frame and also to draw from as broad a knowledge base as possible.

Epistemological Assumptions and Methodology

This book is not a case study, a report, or a history, but an argument. Drawing on Sharon Crowley's and Debra Hawhee's (1999) explanation of ancient rhetoric in the first chapter of their textbook, I would characterize what I do in these pages as an attempt to use both extrinsic rhetorical proofs (facts and testimony) and intrinsic ones (ethos, pathos, and logos, or reason) to advance a course of action in Composition and English Studies. I select facts from both well-known and lesser-known studies, testimony from students, and quotations from those with recognized expertise in language or literacy. I use students' texts and drawings, personal narratives, anecdotes, pathos, reinterpretations of theoretical essays, summaries of selected empirical studies, metaphors, and other figures of speech. This book is a rhetorical stew intended to convince readers to accept its argument: that we should experiment critically with broader, braver conceptions of "knowing," "text," "reading," and "writing."

If I were to describe my mode of inquiry using Stephen M. North's categories from *The Making of Knowledge in Composition* (1987), I would describe some of what I do in these chapters as belonging to the work done by "The Critics." That is, I use a hermaneutical mode of inquiry to investigate "knowledge about the meaning of texts, derived from the act of reading, articulated as critical analysis, and refined by dialectic" (1987, 119). I examine selections of what might be called canonical texts in Composition (well-known articles or books by Janet Emig, Paulo Freire, Lev Vygotsky, and others), and I reinterpret them for what I think the field has missed regarding alternate representational systems. I also dabble in North's "Philosophers" category, accepting his definition as having "the impulse to account for, to frame, critique and analyze the field's fundamental assumptions and beliefs" (1987, 91). Throughout the book, but especially in Chapter 1, I examine and critique Composition's reliance on word-based theories of knowing. I also look at Paulo Freire's reception in this country, but I do not claim to be a disinterested historian.

However, when I look back over my professional life as a whole, not just the ten years since I received my doctorate, I come closest to fitting into North's category of "Practitioners," in that much of my knowledge base comes from my teaching experience. I have been a tutor in one writing center and a director in another. The institutions in which I've worked include a middle school, public and private high schools, a two-year college, a four-year liberal-arts college, and two state universities (one in New York and one in Illinois), and the Rensselaer, New York Girls Club. I've taught every level of student from seventh grade through Ph.D. candidates. I've directed plays—with little kids, as well as high school students, as actors. When I was faculty advisor for a yearbook, I learned and taught layout design. I've tutored algebra and geometry and showed my nephew how to swing a golf club. I've taught composition, creative writing, literary theory, and driver education—not at the same time, though they're not as far apart as one might think.

My students and I have worked with lots of words, but we've also seen knowing and not-knowing manifest themselves in many ways. I've seen how people's bodies reflect both fear and confidence as they've faced opening-night stage fright, road test terrors, and writer's block. I have not fully articulated what my practice reveals about my epistemology, but the struggle to do so, knowing I'm partly unconscious of ideologies shaping my perceptions, challenges me to be as methodologically self-aware as possible. Mostly what I've learned is that I have to keep learning.

Therefore, much of what I "know" is experiential, shot through with composition, literary, critical, and more recently disability studies theory, but also influenced by selected empirical research in neuroscience, biology, and psychology. It should go without saying that assumptions about knowledge in these areas are different, and I am grateful to C. H. Knoblauch and Lil Brannon (1984) for helping me analyze epistemological differences and "true intellectual oppositions" these theories might involve.[5]

In trying to characterize where I fit into published maps of the field, I admit I gather rhetorical proofs from fields with different modes of inquiry and assumptions about what constitutes knowledge. I am inspired, however, by James Berlin's description in *Rhetorics, Poetics, and Cultures* (1996) of social-epistemic rhetoric:

> Social-epistemic rhetoric is self-reflexive, acknowledging its own rhetoricity, its own discursive constitution and limitations. This means that it does not deny its inescapable ideological predispositions, its politically situated condition. It does not claim to be above ideology, a transcendent discourse that objectively adjudicates competing ideological claims. It knows that it is itself ideologically situated, itself an intervention in the political process, as are all rhetorics. Significantly, it contains within it a utopian moment, a conception of the good democratic society and the good life for all of its members. At the same

> time, it is aware of its historical contingency, of its limitations and incompleteness, remaining open to change and revision. (81)

I hope my approach to teaching, inquiry, research, and learning intersects positively with that description.

Theoretical Problems

This book also describes how I or others use sketching, drawing, movement, oral group work, presentations, or performance to stimulate thinking. It suggests how and why we can use non-writing (in addition to writing, of course) to help students write better, even as it questions what "writing better" means and whose interests that writing serves.

As I consider these questions and redesign my courses around multisensory strategies, I need to address some theoretical problems involved. Much of the intellectual work described in these pages involves collaboration: students sketching patterns and explaining them to classmates, working in groups, responding to multiple drafts via e-mail, using 3-D models, presenting or performing in front of a group, etc. A good place to begin is with the juxtaposed essays about collaborative work that appear in Victor Villanueva's *Cross-Talk in Comp Theory* (1997).[6] Drawing on Richard Rorty, Kenneth Bruffee argues that collaboration can result in insightful "abnormal discourse," Rorty's phrase for unconventional commentary coming from an individual in a collaborative group (Rorty 1991, 407). If one group member is from another culture, for example, she or he might offer an "off the wall" take on conventional views. This "abnormal discourse" can force other group members to rethink their positions.

John Trimbur and Greg Myers, however, take issue with Rorty's and Bruffee's faith in abnormal discourse. Myers argues that ideologies are so powerful they prevent a group from offering anything other than a hegemonic agreement on what is appropriate or valuable. To view collaborative work in any way other than as a confirmation of mainstream ideologies, Myers argues, is naive. He says, "In this article, I am asking, not for a new kind of assignment, but for more skepticism about what assignments do to reproduce the structures of our society" (1986, 434).

Similarly, Trimbur criticizes Rorty's idea of "abnormal discourse," arguing that it relies on a "romantic" idea of an individual, a fool or a rebel who somehow resists convention. Instead, Trimbur argues, consensus can be used to "generate differences, and to transform the relations of power that determine who may speak and what counts as a meaningful statement." How consensus and discensus are used, Trimbur says, "depends on the teacher's practice" (1989, 440). Myers and

Trimbur are both wary of Bruffee's use of consensus for its possible role in "accepting the current production and distribution of knowledge and discourse as unproblematical and given" (1989, 448). Trimbur would like to see those discussions of textual analysis framed as questions of power: whose readings, writings, or interpretations are valued and whose are not, as well as why we are doing certain kinds of interpretations in the first place.

Whenever I use the collaborative and/or multisensory work described in this book, which is most of the time, I think about the Rorty, Bruffee, Myers, and Trimbur published debate about consensus, discensus, and whether through my philosophy of teaching I am accepting or challenging oppressive societal practices. What does it mean that I use sketching, movement, peer responding, performance, or collaborative group work to "help students write better"? (And what does "write better" mean?) Am I opposing hegemonic injustices or am I complicit in supporting them? Although I reject the binary, I welcome the dialectic. These questions keep me bothered, keep me thinking about what I'm doing and why. What follows is one attempt to explain where the theories and practices I discuss in this book fit into my life's work. I will return to this question later.

Although there's nothing Myers says that I disagree with, I must finally reject the binary evident in his critique, and it is troublesome that he does not describe what he would have his students *do* that would be consistent with his theoretical stance. But Myers forces me to ask myself, Does my teaching reproduce or critique "the structures of society"? I think, finally, that it must be doing a bit of both. I'm complicit in supporting present societal values, for good or for ill, in that I think it's my job to help students secure a reasonably satisfying career in this society. Most of the students I encounter come to college partly, maybe mostly, to enter a profession, where they will make the money that with luck will pay their bills, including the loans they took to go to college. Therefore, I feel that it is part of my responsibility as a writing teacher to help them approach present and future writing tasks, in or out of college, with confidence, skill, rhetorical savvy, and yes, some healthy skepticism and critique about what our culture seems to value. This latter issue I address when I pick readings that call attention to discrimination, unequal distribution of wealth, and other injustices in our society. However, my main contribution against hegemony is using a multi-modal pedagogy that challenges the unaddressed privileging of those who use written words well, and the conventional discrimination against those whose talents involve other representational systems.

Therefore, I try to teach students, or help them to learn, effective rhetorical strategies. If they can recognize them in other people's writing, they will be less at the mercy of others' rhetorical power. As

Crowley and Hawhee put it, "the critical capacity conferred by rhetoric can free its students from the manipulative rhetoric of others" (1999, 4). In another sense, I hope I am opposing injustices by helping students recognize and use powerful language. If they can use rhetorical strategies effectively in their own writing, perhaps they can convince their world-mates to be more just, ethical people. I tell students that having rhetorical power does not mean that they will use it for "good" purposes, but that I hope any newfound power they get from this class they will use to improve the world, not make it worse. How to address questions of ethics—ethically—in the classroom is a problem I continuously revisit.

There are at least three strong reasons to use multiple, alternate strategies to teach writing. First, because words are so powerful, we must use all available means to help students discover the power of words and their own power to use them. As Robert Scholes wrote, "Textual power is ultimately power to change the world" (1985, 165). Second, we must reach as many students as possible and we must help them reach their full potential. Third, and at the very least, we must "do no harm." Using multiple ways of knowing also addresses a pedagogical injustice that is both systemic and local. Throughout most of the educational system, and especially in writing classes, students are forced to use linguisto-centric tools to perform virtually all intellectual tasks.

Composition is partly failing on all three counts. We are not using all available means of helping students realize and use the power of written text. We are relying too much on linguistic pathways, probably because that's our preferred inroad, and we're not taking full advantage of what students can teach us about oral, spatial, visual, social, or other ways of knowing. Therefore, we are excluding people. In addition, the linguistically talented students who tell us they "love English" are not developing as much as they could be as thinkers because they (and we) are missing the insights from pathways others could show us. Finally, we might be doing harm, albeit inadvertently, to students who know things in ways we do not. They fail our courses, but it is we who are failing them. We are disrespecting their other intellectual contributions, even as we are losing what they could teach us.

So what, finally, are the epistemological assumptions behind "multiple channel" strategies? Let me address that question through an epistemological map of the field. In "Rhetorical Constructions" (1988), C. H. Knoblauch divides assumptions about knowledge and language into "four distinct views" of the "ground" or basis for verbal meaning. In the "ontological" quadrant, language is not related to knowledge except as a representation of thought. In this view, "truth" or "reality" exist prior to language, and language has no power to change either. The "objectivist" view of knowledge and language began in the seventeenth century with an emphasis on observable, experiential, "scientific" facts. The third view is "expressionist," locating knowledge in human consciousness and individual imagination. The fourth view Knoblauch calls "the dialogical or sociological statement," which "rejects at once the metaphysics of an ontological argument, the positivist, reifying tendencies of objectivist rhetoric, and the privileging of 'consciousness' (universally or individually conceived), associated with expressionist rhetoric." In this sociological quadrant, "Language is regarded as a social practice rooted, as are all social practices, in material and historical process" (Knoblauch 1988, 134).

How do my assumptions about knowledge and language fit into those quadrants, and what do the multiple approaches I use indicate about my assumptions? Critics may view some of these strategies as expressionistic in that the tasks seem to assume if writers think about their texts carefully enough, or from enough distance, that they will find "true" meaning and revise accordingly. However, what students are "seeing" in that metacognitive distance is shaped by socially constructed factors: the expectations of a discourse community, the different ways a variety of readers will receive their texts, the intertextual and connotative meaning of a particular word, the cultural work they want their text to do. Sometimes, promoting any way of knowing may seem to assume an ontologically "right" way of teaching. While I do not believe in one right way to teach everyone, and I have stopped looking for it, I do think there are wrongheaded, potentially harmful things we do that we ought to change. While I am aware that scientific-objectivist research has methodological flaws and is typically not sufficiently aware of the rhetorical nature of its own reporting, I do not reject all of it out of hand. To adapt Elbow's phrase, I try to believe it and doubt it at once, trying to fit it into my own, ever-shifting epistemological frame. Am I inconsistent? Yes. Do I confuse my students? I hope so, but productively, I think.

I'm still working through my philosophy of teaching because I'm still working through my philosophy of life. I think it may not be necessary or even possible to ground knowledge making in only one quadrant. My view of knowledge and language is not yet fixed. It is partly experiential, from years as a practitioner, and partly ontological, from indelible years of Catholic school religion classes that were both sublime and ridiculous. I know things also from what I read: fiction, newspapers, student work, and composition articles—also alternately sublime and ridiculous.

Personally, I don't "know" that there is not an ontological basis for meaning. I think I believe that knowledge is grounded partly in all four quadrants. That's contradictory perhaps, but only according to a kind of logic that is arguably irrelevant in a postmodern world in which the only certain thing is its contradictory nature. I know, mostly from background in feminist theory (thanks to graduate classes from Judith Fetterley and Joan Schulz at SUNY Albany), that what a society accepts as "known" is socially constructed. I see how women and others in this culture have been constructed, and I know that this construction is unjust and unnatural—the latter term also a social construction. A good part of what I "know" comes from my life experiences and observations, even though what I "see" and "experience" is always already filtered through a socially constructed lens. Nevertheless, my experiences seem real to me, and I live my present life under the influence of my past, aware that my notion of "self" as a subject in a post-modern world is something Lester Faigley (1995) has effectively problematized. I realize my epistemological assumptions contradict one another. Some days I dwell more in one mode of inquiry, one quadrant of assumptions, than in another. I can live with the confusion. I welcome it, in fact, often discussing these theoretical conflicts with my students, the majority of whom are planning to be teachers who also need to examine their view of knowledge.

The students in my classes live in a world in which epistemologies compete and overlap, in a world of people whose beliefs are shaped by different and various assumptions about knowledge and power. Assumptions in the field of Composition about writing are also socially constructed, complicated by Composition's vested interest in promoting the idea that knowledge is word-based. If students can generate knowledge from drawing as much as they can discover it from writing, our expertise in writing may be less valued.

It matters whether we think knowledge comes from an ontological source, inner selves, "science," or sociological dialectic because these assumptions impact whether people think there's a "natural way" things are or whether they can change the "reality" their society has constructed. But why can't those different epistemological systems oppose each other cooperatively? So what if they contradict each other? If they didn't, then we would "know" once and for all that we're right, which would be itself a kind of essentializing position. So we should not only live with the contradictions but encourage them. Everything we "know," all that is "real," we interpret through a socially constructed lens. We can also "know" things through our lives, or because we've read a well-done piece of research, or even because we "believe" it on some level through what remains of ontological beliefs.

We need to start with practice and we need to start with theory. We need to start with assumptions, with the various definitions of "writing" that emerge when we use that word and think we're all talking about the same thing when we're not. The words, sentences, essays, novels, poems that appear on a page or screen are the result of complex sociological, emotional, physical, and neurological processes that none of us completely understands. The "writing process" of early drafting, getting responses, revising, and editing is a logical, workable pedagogical approach, especially for English teachers who probably themselves compose written drafts as part of their own preferred process. But it is not the only approach.

This book will privilege speaking and listening, drawing and moving, along with writing and reading, as ways of making knowledge. The theoretical assumptions of the practice described may not always be consistent. Because I draw multi-modal strategies from so many different epistemological backgrounds, I may be accused of using what Knoblauch and Brannon call "a smorgasbord theory of instruction" (1984, 15). Part of me agrees with them that using contradictory theories can be risky and confusing for students. However, conflicting views of knowledge should confuse us, as well as our students, providing we point to the conflicts and discuss the consequences of their differences. If we are aware of contradictions, they can keep us on our intellectual toes, keep us rethinking and requestioning what we do and why. Having a consistent theoretical base, a sure epistemology may be consistent, but it carries with it the danger that we will become too sure, too comfortable with what we do in our classes, too sure that the way we think knowledge gets made and writing gets done, is the only or best way. Learning comes from surprise, doubt, and confusion. We, as well as our students, can handle unanswered questions about what we're doing and why. In fact, we should foreground those questions more often than we do.

Chapter Summaries

Chapter 1 challenges current ways of knowing foregrounded in most writing and English classes, calling into question the continued privileging of written texts as having the primary role in the production of knowledge. I reinterpret a selection of influential Composition theorists, and I critique baseline assumptions about knowledge making in our discipline. I briefly survey what people both inside and outside Composition have said about knowledge making beyond word-based approaches, and I explain why most of them have not been taken seriously in our field.

Chapter 2 focuses on Paulo Freire's reception in Composition: what has been privileged, what has been marginalized. While I do not argue "against" what has been taken from Freire and used in North American Composition classes, I do argue that an important part of Freire's praxis that has not been foregrounded is his use of what he called "multiple channels of communication."

Chapter 3 will foreground other, more intellectually diverse and challenging ways of knowing than are currently emphasized in most Composition and English Studies classrooms. It will show how aural, visual, kinesthetic, spatial, and social approaches can challenge students and teachers alike to think beyond text-based theory and practice and help writers generate and reconceptualize ideas. It can help them gain a metacognitive distance on their work so far, or see it from a different perspective. If those with talents other than linguistic ones can take advantage of what they do well, if they can find a way to use their spatial or physical or musical or artistic interests in their writing habits, they may like writing more and be better at it. If already-good writers are expected to work outside their linguistic comfort zone, to reconceive their project in alternate representations, the challenge of doing so may give them insights, approaches, or metaphors that will inform their work on more sophisticated levels. This chapter includes much student work demonstrating or describing alternate strategies and how students used them to help generate and organize writing projects. I use their work not as detailed case studies, but as brief examples of what some students did in one place and time, using non-writing strategies as they generated and honed their ideas and revised their drafts. It is meant to spark reflection, not imitation.[7]

Chapter 4 addresses revising and editing issues. It first critiques how "grammar" and "correctness" are usually framed in this culture, and then it provides some examples of how multisensory approaches can help writers deal with issues that are "simple" only to those with certain kinds of linguistic talents or cultural capital. Revising and editing, it should go without saying, cannot be neatly separated from generating and organizing issues discussed in the last chapter. Nor can revising and editing, or generating and organizing, be separated from the theoretical, ideological, and material forces that shape where, when, how, and with whom they take place. I could have separated issues related to writing by theorist, by historical circumstances, by location along a political continuum, or by alphabet. But I have separated them this way, with revising and editing in this chapter, because when I bring students through a writing project, I usually don't talk about editing strategies until late in the project—though it might be fun some time to do so first.

Chapter 5 has some brief suggestions about how alternate approaches might be used to enhance the *reading* of texts, in addition to the writing of them. I summarize other people's good ideas in this regard, as well as some of my own, and how and why I use them in my classes.

Chapter 6 serves as a point of departure for ways to frame discussions of what we are doing when we use these strategies, and why. To put it bluntly, if and when we are asked to justify our use of what others will characterize as "non-rigorous" approaches, because they involve non-writing, we may need some powerful rhetorical spin to explain our theory and practice.

Talking, Sketching, Moving challenges teacher/scholars and students in Composition and English Studies to expect more of themselves and each other. It proposes a shift in theoretical assumptions about "reading" and "writing," and it describes unconventional classroom practices that emerge from serious reflection on that theoretical shift.

Notes

1. In separate presentations, both Gross and Eriksson talked about Darwin's Tree of Life sketch at the 1999 Fourth National Writing Across the Curriculum Conference at Cornell University, Ithaca, NY, June 1999.

2. See Gardner's *Frames of Mind* (1983) for explanations of the first seven. See Kathy Checkley's interview with Gardner in the September 1997 *Educational Leadership* for a good explanation of all eight.

3. Ironically, Howard Gardner's multiple intelligence theory is used in many secondary "gifted and talented" programs. See Reid and Romanoff (1997) and Fulkerson and Horvich (1998).

4. I am not related to that family of Dunns.

5. See page 5 in their *Rhetorical Traditions* and also Knoblauch's (1988) "Rhetorical Constructions: Dialogue and Commitment."

6. Many of the essays cited in this book I revisited because of Victor Villanueva's excellent collection, *Cross-Talk in Comp Theory,* as well as Mark Wiley, Barbara Gleason, and Louise Wetherbee Phelps' excellent collection, *Composition in Four Keys*. I am grateful to all of them for making such important essays easily accessible. In my discussion of the "abnormal discourse" debate, the page numbers in parentheses refer to the Villanueva collection.

7. I have institutional permission to conduct research, and all students whose work is included here have been informed that I might use their work in this book. They have signed permission slips from my university's Institutional Research Board as well as from this publisher. I have changed their names, as I told them I would, unless they indicated in writing on their permission slips that they wanted their real or full names used, in which case I have complied with their wishes.

Chapter One

Challenging Theories
of Knowing

Words, words, words.

—Hamlet

The word *challenging* in the title of this chapter should be read as both a verb and an adjective. First we need *to challenge* theories of knowing that privilege only one way of conceiving ideas. Then we need to develop *challenging* pedagogies that use and develop alternate literacies, that expect the most from us and our students.

It may seem at first absurd to question an over-emphasis on writing in a discipline whose raison d'être is, like no other discipline, for and about writing. That common-sense assumption, however, may be what makes it so difficult for us in Composition to see word-based pedagogies in any way other than supportive of learning.[1] Generally speaking, Composition believes that writing is not simply *one* way of knowing; it is *the* way. In Composition theory courses, readings attest mostly to writing's benefits. That commonplace may be what makes it so difficult for us in Composition to see word-based epistemologies in any way other than liberatory and promoting of social justice. A sampling of our most influential theorists will give a sense of how many Compositionists view the role written language plays in making knowledge. The first three are from essays that appear in Victor Villanueva's *Cross-Talk in Comp-Theory* (1997), a popular anthology.

- "Rather than truth being prior to language, language is prior to truth and determines what shape truth can take" (243). This is part of James Berlin's summary in "Contemporary Composition" of what he calls the New Rhetoric, which he says is "the most intelligent and most practical alternative available, serving in every way the best interests of our students" (234).

- "Without the word there is no world" (462). That statement is from Charles Schuster's summary of Mikhail Bakhtin's view of speaking and writing, which, Schuster argues, supports "the *primacy of language* as the means by which we conceive the world" (my emphasis, 461).

- In "Cognition, Convention, and Certainty," Patricia Bizzell contrasts two main "camps" in Composition: (1) the "inner-directed" theorists who focus on the individual, seek universal writing processes, and support a "standard" language; and (2) the "outer-directed" theorists, some of whom would say that "one learns to think only by learning a language, and one can't have an idea one doesn't have a word for" (367–71).

This second, "outer-directed" view of language-as-determiner-of-thought structure, as Bizzell points out, was greatly influenced by the Sapir-Whorf hypothesis, and she recommends Adam Schaff's description of it, part of which is as follows:

1. Language is a social product. The language system in which we are educated, and in which we think, shapes the way we perceive the world around us.

2. In view of the differences between the various language systems, people thinking in different languages perceive the world in different ways. These differences of language are reflections of the different environments that produce them (1973, 62).

This ethnolinguistic hypothesis of the 1930s rejects by implication the theories of the "inner-directed" camp Bizzell described above. It explains how people's ideological assumptions regarding time, reality, gender, etc., are shaped by, and also shape, language. If this hypothesis is sound, we cannot teach "universal" rules about language; we cannot get beyond language. Here are more statements about language that support "the primacy of language."

Drawing on Locke, Descartes, and Kant, C. H. Knoblauch and Lil Brannon make the point in *Rhetorical Traditions and the Teaching of Writing* (1984) that language is not (as they say the ancient rhetoricians believed) the dress of thought. Rather, "discourse makes knowledge . . ." (57). They do leave the door open for other ways of knowing besides language: "All human beings share and apply the competence to make meaning through symbolic representation, including language" (61). However, what their book ultimately stresses is that "knowledge is a linguistic construction, a 'discourse.' Knowing is an activity of creating and shaping 'texts,' just as Descartes had implied, not an absolute state or condition" (55). This creating and shaping can happen "through discourse, linguistic or otherwise" (54), but they do not discuss the "otherwise." They point out John Locke's associating "the active character of the mind" with how people interpret experience (55), but their book on the teaching of writing focuses almost exclusively in manifestations of that active mind in discourse, language, and words.

Ann E. Berthoff's attention to meaning making has also had a profound influence on our field. In the Preface to *Reclaiming the Imagination* (1984), she names language as the most important intellectual tool: "those learning to write and to teach writing will discover that language is itself the great heuristic." And Walter Ong, who is perhaps the strongest and most controversial promoter of written language being superior to the oral form, writes, "Orally managed language and thought is not noted for analytic precision" (1987, 104).

"The Primacy of Language"

Although it seems clear that language structures are determined by and help determine ideologies, there is more to meaning making than linguistic structures. If we continue to focus on language as "the great heuristic," we should at least make as honest an effort as we can to examine our ideological base, as well as our possible vested interest in those beliefs.

In the same way the Sapir-Whorf hypothesis explains how language both shapes and is shaped by ideological assumptions, Composition's bag of evidence is filled with theories and methodological approaches that are shaped by, and shape, our beliefs about language and learning. Our beliefs about what it means to know, spring from and toward the theorists and theories we select to support our claims. This is true for every field and is not a criticism. However, since we have gotten into the business of analyzing the underlying assumptions in the discourses of other disciplines, we should continue Composition's admirable past efforts to be self-reflexive and examine the assumptions supporting our own. Compositionists seem to hold views of language so deeply that we take for granted its place on the top rung of the meaning-making ladder.

Drawing on Marxist definitions, Greg Myers uses the term *ideology* "to describe the whole system of thought and belief that goes with a social and economic system, the thoughts that structure our thinking so deeply that we take them for granted, as the nature of the real world" (1986, 156). What we must acknowledge in the social and economic system of Composition are the commonplaces informing our own view of "truth," even if we are careful not to use that word. Composition should view its worship of the written word, its assumptions regarding "the primacy of language," not as a given, but as itself an ideology. Our whole system of thought privileges written language as the best and most powerful way of thinking. One example can be seen in Villanueva's *Cross-Talk in Comp Theory*, where Janet Emig's (1977) "Writing as a Mode of Learning" appears in a section of the table of contents called "The 'Given' in Our Conversations: The Writing Process." This ideology regarding "the great heuristic" affects our preference for certain kinds of methodologies and certain kinds of theorists. It helps explain why we pick and choose who to cite and foreground.

It's not that Composition has completely ignored alternate ways of knowing. Within our own field, this idea has surfaced fairly often. It's just that it seems never to be taken seriously for very long. Ira Shor, Henry Giroux, bell hooks, Sharon Crowley, and others have pointed out (and critiqued the idea) that written language is unfairly privileged in school. Gerald Washington (1996) points to the "*different* cognitive tasks" students undertake when they use oral forms of communication. He argues further that "composition teachers can use this *alternative* manner of communication as a starting point for the teaching of writing skills" (his emphasis, 429). He also points out that for this to happen, "teacher attitudes" would first have to change. Donna LeCourt (1996), in "WAC as Critical Pedagogy: The Third Stage?" critiques most contemporary Writing Across the Curriculum programs for not paying enough attention to cultural critique or to "alternative literacies and other ways of knowing" (390).

Eleanor Kutz and Hepzibah Roskelly in *An Unquiet Pedagogy* (1991) call for "a reinvented curriculum" (310) in which teachers would "Allow other ways of knowing into the classroom" (115).[2] Karen Klein and Linda Hecker (1994) have worked with kinesthetics and teaching writing. More recently, Pam Childers, Eric Hobson, and Joan Mullin have used art as a pathway to learning and writing in their book, *ARTiculating Writing: Teaching Writing in a Visual World*. As will be discussed in Chapter 5, Peter Smagorinsky has done much work with Gardner's multiple intelligences at the secondary level, and Dan Kirby, Tom Liner, and Ruth Vinz in their book *Inside Out* also suggest multisensory approaches for teaching English in the schools. In addition, there was an entire issue of *English Journal* devoted to teaching with multiple intelligences, though the reaction to ideas discussed in that journal was predictively mixed, as we shall see in Chapter 6.

Whether an alternate conception of knowing comes from outside or inside Composition, it is an idea that has not been fully pursued or taken seriously in our field. Look in composition classrooms and you will see some group work and oral discussion. You may occasionally see people using art, film, or music. But what you will mostly see in composition classes are activities linked to "the primacy of language," especially writing, as a "unique" heuristic for thinking: students doing written drafts, written responses to peers, written reading journals, written reading logs, freewriting, written memos or metacognitive analyses, written outlines, or written online chats.

This focus on writing may partly account for the initial reception, and current foundering, of the Writing Across the Curriculum movement. It may partly account for why, as a field, we have not embraced research on voice-to-type word processing programs. It may partly explain why our rhetorical proofs lean heavily on testimony from people we as a field have invested with a kind of agreed-upon authority about language and learning (Berlin, Britton, Emig, etc.), as well as our use of theorists coming from, or influenced by, literary studies (Bahktin, Derrida, Foucault, Vygotksy, etc.).[3] It's not that these theorists are never taken to task for something, but they are cited over and over in our field (as in this book, for example), the assumption being that their research and/or ideas are so respected that sometimes a quotation alone from one of them is enough support for a claim.

In a field that prides itself on its theoretical awareness, many of us in Composition believe we hold radical critiques of hegemonic worldviews. However, we are sometimes quite conventional in our acceptance of either/or judgments regarding empirical research (positivist and essentialist), non-language-based theories of learning (romantic or sentimental), and any philosophy of life that is not 100 percent social constructivist (naive or untheoretical).

We are also quite conventional in our apparent acceptance of dominant views that written language is the most important indicator of intellectual sophistication. Composition is justly proud of its tradition of asking questions, of welcoming dialectic. To continue that tradition, we need to more fully articulate the implications of "the primacy of language."

The Backstory to "The Primacy of Language"

The social construction of knowledge is another commonplace of our field. As Lester Faigley observes in *Fragments of Rationality*, "In the 1980s, much of composition theory came to assume that knowledge is socially constructed and rhetorical in nature, a development attributable to the impact of postmodern theory" (1995, 15). This is not to say that every Composition teacher/scholar subscribes to this view, but it seems no longer necessary to argue, at the Conference on College Composition and Communication (CCCC) or in *College Composition and Communication* (CCC), for example, that ideology shapes perception.

James Berlin's view of language and "verbal constructs" as an exclusive way of knowing is well known. Here is Berlin, also anthologized in *Cross-Talk in Comp Theory*, on the worldview he supports, "social-epistemic rhetoric":

> For social-epistemic rhetoric, the real is located in a relationship that involves the dialectical interaction of the observer, the discourse community (social group) in which the observer is functioning, and the material conditions of existence. Knowledge is never found in any one of these but can only be posited as a product of the dialectic in which all three come together. (More of this in a moment.) Most important, this dialectic is grounded in language: *the observer, the discourse community, and the material conditions of existence are all verbal constructs.* This does not mean that the three do not exist apart from language: they do. *This does mean that we cannot talk and write about them—indeed, we cannot know them—apart from language.* (my emphasis, in Villanueva 1997, 692–93)

Berlin is right, of course, that we cannot talk or write about the observer, the discourse community, or the material conditions of existence without language. That we cannot "know them" without language is more troublesome, unless his view of "language" includes all symbol systems, all ways of conceiving of and representing ideas. However, many in Composition seem to have taken a narrow, literal view of social-epistemic rhetoric: that there is no way of "knowing" anything beyond "verbal constructs," and no way of representing a dialectic "apart from language." This impoverished view of what counts as legitimate intellectual activity, limiting it to that which involves "verbal constructs," explains our underuse of alternate representational systems.

This restrictive construction of how people make meaning may also be due to who "we" are, and our discourse community's constructed circular logic that resists intersections with non-verbal representational systems. The "we" who "cannot know" dialectic "apart from language" are, after all, Composition specialists and English professors. We are talkers, readers, and writers: people whose ways of knowing *are* grounded primarily in "verbal constructs," and whose ways of knowing have been rewarded by the very socially constructed privileges to which Berlin says we should pay more attention.

Mikhail Bakhtin is another oft-quoted theorist, whose words are powerful rhetorical proofs. His influence can be seen in theoretical articles in both Literary Studies and Composition. However, we need to examine our assumptions behind the power we bestow on Bakhtin's writings. Bakhtin was a literary theorist, as Charles Schuster points out (in Villanueva 1997, 457), and Composition, housed as it mostly still is in English departments, has a strong historical association with literary and critical theory. Composition was born into an institutional culture that has a reverence not only for words, but for interpretations of words, as Stephen North points out (1987, 116). By celebrating and demonstrating the power of written language, we by extension promote our power to use, teach, and interpret writing. Therefore, we need to be aware of the possibility that we are, perhaps unconsciously, privileging theories and theorists that link thought and language.

Here is more of Schuster's anthologized interpretation of Bakhtin. Imagine a person not talented with language hearing this:

> Without the word there is no world. Language is not just a bridge between "I" and "Thou," it *is* "I" and "Thou." *Language is thus fundamental not only to learning but to mind; it both creates and is created by the human intelligence.* When we speak and write, we create ourselves and the world. *No intellectual construct—no expression or idea—can exist without language*, and language is itself continuously interactive in its nature. (my emphasis, in Villanueva 1997, 462)

This linking of language use with intelligence is a double-edged sword. Fusing language and human meaning making supports the importance of studying language and teaching writing. However, we need to be aware that we are professionally and financially invested in privileging something we're announcing as "the primacy of language." We also need to be aware of a more troubling aspect of this privileging. Even if it is unspoken, there is an implied corollary in this announcement regarding lack of language skills, lack of intelligence—or even lack of humanness.

An analogous situation in American fiction is useful here. In "The War Prayer," Mark Twain's "aged stranger" articulates for oblivious churchgoers the "unspoken" prayer: what they must *also* be asking for when they send their loved ones off to war. The point is that as the people explicitly pray for victory and glory, and for the safety of their own army, they are implicitly praying for the destruction of their enemy's cities and the agony and death of its soldiers, who are also being sent off to war by their loving families. The pale man with long white hair enters the church, walks to the pulpit, and says aloud that unspoken prayer, the cruel underside of the noble-sounding victory prayer:

> —for our sakes who adore Thee, Lord, blast their hopes, blight their lives, protract their bitter pilgrimage, make heavy their steps, water

their way with their tears, stain the white snow with the blood of their wounded feet! We ask it, in the spirit of love, . . . (1983, 425)

Similarly, there is an unspoken prayer, or at least an unspoken backstory, to our enthusiastic promotion of language-as-indicator-of-intelligence, even of humanness.

Brenda Jo Brueggemann's (1999) discussion of deafness and rhetoric is relevant to this discussion. In a section of *Lend Me Your Ear: Rhetorical Constructions of Deafness* called "The Other Half of the Dialogue," Brueggemann traces the link between rhetoric and constructions of deafness back several millennia, but focuses on the Age of Reason. She reconstitutes the implied enthymeme that must explain why deaf education was the first "special education," the need to make children more "human" by giving them language: "And in this age, Reason was, of course the essence of being human. The syllogism created—rhetorical, faulty, and enthymematic as it is—sounds like this: *Language is human; speech is language; therefore, deaf people are inhuman, and deafness is a problem*" (her emphasis, 11).

Brueggemann's critique of the view that people who could not hear were not human without language/speech is applicable in Composition's worshipping of language, especially the written word. Her syllogism about deafness might be extended to a parallel syllogism about illiteracy:

Language is human.

Writing is language.

Therefore those who cannot write are less human.

This is the sword's other edge: the implication, the backstory, of our emphasis on writing. This is what we, at least most of us, do not say or consciously think. That implied episteme, however, may be absorbed by our students as the logical extension of our focus on writing-as-knowing, unless we also embrace non-language-based ways of knowing.

Other Ways of Knowing

"You can't describe it in words. Your fingers just find the right places."
—Brian Wilson on how he writes his songs[4]

Perhaps more than one thing is possible. Language reflects and shapes our thinking, but our thinking can also go to another room and play with things that precede or go beyond words. Here is dyslexic teacher Donald E. Lyman's answer to the question of how he thought as a child:

I thought, to the best of my recollection, in strong visual images. Quite simply, I pictured in my mind what I had just done and what I planned to do next. What I was doing, I simply did. A kind of sensory motor intelligence, a "body knowing," guided me. You have experienced a similar knowing when you served a tennis ball, typed a letter, diapered a baby, or danced the night away. We all know that directing such activities with words causes a sudden drop in performance. (1986, 25)

Howard Gardner's work on "multiple intelligences" is well known, as is Daniel Goleman's emphasis on what he calls "emotional intelligence": "such as being able to motivate oneself and persist in the face of frustrations; to control impulse and delay gratification; to regulate one's moods and keep distress from swamping the ability to think; to emphasize and to hope" (1995, 34). In neuroscience, Antonio R. Damasio has shown the role emotions play in thinking. He rejects the idea that language alone produces consciousness and knowing: "Language—that is, words and sentences—is a translation of something else, a conversion from nonlinguistic images which stand for entities, events, relationships, and inferences" (1999, 107).

Many people have described their thinking process as visual, not verbal. In his book on visual thinking, *In the Mind's Eye*, Thomas G. West (1997) argues that many scientists and mathematicians through history have been gifted visual thinkers. West points out that James Gleick's work in chaos theory focuses on "visual modes of thought and analysis" (36). West defines visual thinking as "that form of thought in which images are generated or recalled in the mind and are manipulated, overlaid, translated, associated with other similar forms (as with a metaphor), rotated, increased or reduced in size, distorted, or otherwise transformed from one familiar image into another" (21). West observes that the talent for visual thinking is sometimes concomitant with difficulties with other types of learning, especially perhaps the linear, word-based learning that is typical of English Studies curricula. He names many people who were on the fringes of their disciplines, not whopping successes in their contemporary mainstream professions, who had a profound effect on their field in the long term.

West argues that substantial, creative breakthroughs in physics, math, and chemistry were due to visual or spatial insights of people such as Michael Faraday, a scientist from the early 19th century, who did groundbreaking work in the field of electromagnetics. West says scientists are "ambivalent" toward Faraday, who was not a mathematician but a philosopher and scientist. Another visual thinker West names is Karl Pearson, who (with his son, E. S. Pearson) in the nineteenth century, was the first "to apply statistics systematically to biological phenomena" (1997, 34). West suggests that sometimes those who are most successful, most invested, most entrenched in a scientific field, are the ones with the most at stake, the most to lose should they pursue a line of thinking not in strict accord with conventional wisdom in that field. As an example, he uses a nineteenth-century British physicist, William Thompson (Lord Kelvin), whose name is on the absolute zero temperature scale. Kelvin "proved" that people were incapable of flight. His calculations were correct, and he used logically the principles of physics known at that time. West suggests Kelvin's very certainty about things prevented him from having creative insights. Michael Faraday, on the other hand, was never fully accepted into the mainstream profession. But perhaps he had less to lose than Kelvin did by being unsure, by taking chances.

West's main point is that we may be wasting some of our best minds by forcing them into frameworks of thinking and communicating that slow them down. In fact, West suggests that "the conventional beliefs on which our educational system and major institutions are based may be fundamentally flawed" (40). We need the outside-the-box thinking that visual thinkers can do. They might have trouble seeing the intricacies of the part, but they can clearly see the whole. They can synthesize and analyze quickly. They seize a global vision of a system at once, manipulate it, turn it around, and look at it from different perspectives—all inside their heads. They can visualize solutions long before they can explain them easily in words to their colleagues.

The irony, and tragedy, of this kind of thinking, says West, is that sometimes the most insightful mathematicians, who relish the complex, sophisticated problems of advanced, theoretical mathematics, perform poorly in the arithmetic-based, lower levels of math. Their poor performance in the early years of school puts them on a non-academic track, making it difficult for them to ever get to the part of math or physics in which they could excel.

What if there is a parallel irony in English? What if some students who have the most difficulty with one level of writing—with surface correctness, for example—have complex, sophisticated ideas, but their "grammar" problems peg them as "basic writers," slot them in a lower academic track, and wring out of them any confidence they might have had about themselves or any enthusiasm they might have had for learning? What harm could come from having greater expectations for these students?

Critics of stories describing Faraday's early difficulties with school say, perhaps rightly so, that these famous geniuses are being romanticized.[5] However, the many excerpts West cites of these people's letters and journals indicate that their minds worked in pictures, three-dimensional models, graphs, etc. Perhaps it is we in Composition who romanticize other forms of symbols—alphabetic ones. Perhaps it is we who have an artificial notion that sophisticated thought can only happen in "verbal constructs."

Not every person who has trouble reading and writing is an Albert Einstein, Charles Darwin, or Michael Faraday. But dominant assumptions about language and learning in our writing programs may be greatly underestimating the intellectual potential of some groups forced to hear about "the great heuristic" (language) that just happens to cater to the talent and learning preference of the person teaching the course. If that doesn't bother us enough to change things, we should realize that we are unquestionably wasting the brain power and the potential insights of people who can visualize things we cannot, who can grasp concepts we cannot, who can solve problems we cannot. If we don't revolutionize learning for the sake of those foundering in a stubborn, restrictive pedagogy, we should do it for ourselves.

One woman's unique ability to think in images has contributed greatly to reform the meat industry's treatment of animals destined for the slaughterhouse. As Oliver Sacks explains in *An Anthropologist on Mars*, Temple Grandin has transformed the experience of beef cattle going to their deaths from a terrifying experience to one that is as humane and calming as possible under the circumstances. An autistic person who thinks in vivid pictures, Grandin uses her visual thinking to reform the cruel, stress-inducing physical path cattle take on their way through a slaughterhouse. Reasoning that euthanized animals should experience a less-stressful death than they might in the wild, Grandin designed ramps and conveyor belts so that the cattle feel no stress or pain as they go to the stun-gun-like machine that makes them unconscious as they go to their deaths. While her extreme form of visual thinking has hindered her in other areas of her life, it enables her to "see" every image each animal sees on its way through the process:

> She designs the most elaborate facilities in her mind, visualizing every component of the system, juxtaposing them in different ways, viewing them from different angles, from near and far. Once the design is complete, she will "run a simulation" in her mind—that is, imagine the entire plant in operation. This simulation may show an unexpected problem, and when this happens she will pinpoint the problem, modify the design, do another simulation—several simulations, if need be—until the design is perfect. Only now, when all is clear in her mind, does she make an actual blueprint of it. (Sacks 1995, 283)

Grandin anticipates and eliminates what would be for the cattle startling images or sudden, stress-inducing movements, so that their final moments are made as quiet and dignified as possible. While Temple

Grandin's extreme form of imagistic thinking might be rare in a typical classroom, it is crucial that teachers are aware of, and know how to nourish and appreciate, the visual thinking talents of their students. Failing to do so may cause bright people to think ill of themselves or to drop courses that reward only one intellectual pathway: writing. Focusing so narrowly on only one way of knowing not only squanders the thinking power of those who flee such a system as soon as they can, but a linguistic-based pedagogy also limits the insights even conventionally "good students" (good writers) may have if challenged to think outside their intellectual comfort zones.

Rhetorical Analysis, Cultural and Literary Criticism, and Epistemological Assumptions

Through rhetorical analysis, scholars in Composition and Rhetoric have demonstrated how language used in other disciplines both reflects (and helps determine) epistemological assumptions in proofs and evidence (Myers, Bazerman, Halloran, Fahnestock, Secor). For example, as both Susan McLeod and Gerald Graff (1997) have pointed out, a simple discourse convention such as verb tense indicates disciplinary beliefs about knowledge. "Presumably, Plato speaks in the present in literary and philosophical contexts because ideas there are considered timeless; only when we move over to history does it start to matter that the writer is dead" (154).[6] Similarly, as others have noted, Modern Language Association (MLA) and American Psychological Association (APA) differences are not just about commas and periods. APA stresses the currency of the research in question—thus they front the publication date and dispense with authors' first names. In addition, many scientific reports have a parade of collaborators. In contrast, MLA puts the date last, foregrounding instead the (usually individual) author's complete name. This is not a simple editorial difference. This MLA citation method used in English Studies reflects the humanistic tradition of foregrounding what individual human beings have written down in words. We also foreground those individuals who link thought and language. We do not have the same interest in drawing attention to those who link thought and image, or thought and emotion, or thought and movement. Our rhetorical proofs come not from a test tube, but from words about words.

If we were to do a rhetorical analysis of our own evidentiary habits of mind, we might be more aware and forthcoming about our own proclivities and vested interests. We might find that we privilege and promote the "primacy of language" ideology through the writings of like-minded people. I think we would also find that our arguments and interpretations have a healthy sprinkling of what Jeanne Fahnestock and Marie Secor saw in their rhetorical analysis of selected literary criticism published between 1978 and 1982: the "appearance/reality" trope, the heading they credit Chaim Perelman and Lucie Olbechts-Tyteca with providing. They say this "dualism" was "the most prevalent special topos" of the literary arguments they studied (84). The argument involves

> the perception of two entities: one more immediate, the other latent; one on the surface, the other deep; one obvious, the other the object of the search. We might even claim that the appearance reality topos is the fundamental assumption of criticism, since without it there would be no impetus to analyze or interpret literature. (1991, 85)

In other words, the literary criticism they analyzed (which they see not as argument at all but as epideictic rhetoric) provides a kind of tour of what lies "beneath" obvious "surface" meanings. Considering Fahnestock's and Secor's analysis that much literary criticism is based on a spatial metaphor of looking beneath the surface, we might say that rhetorical analysis, some kinds of composition theory, and cultural criticism are all different versions of this "beneath-the-surface" searching.

For example, we take delight in pointing out the (hidden?) assumptions of those writing in other disciplines. In the following passage, taken from Barbara Gleason's introduction to the "Key of Science" in *Composition in Four Keys* (1996), the Composition anthology she edited with Mark Wiley and Louise Wetherbee Phelps, she points out the importance of underlying assumptions informing a research agenda. Note the underlying spatial metaphor here (see, I'm doing it, too!), the kind Fahnestock and Secor point out is part of the spatialness of literary criticism

> It is in fact important for us as readers of scientific reports and arguments to be as aware of researchers' assumptions and theories as we are of their findings and conclusions. In reading Janet Emig's 1971 study of twelfth graders' composing processes, for instance, **we discover** Emig not just investigating composing *but advancing the relatively new theory that writing is a process.* **Careful readings** of the other research studies in this section **will reveal** each author's initial questions, premises, or hypotheses to be important indicators of these researchers' theories about writing, writing development, or teaching. (italics Gleason's, boldings mine, 257)

We also take delight in pointing out the naivete of those writing in other disciplines. Victor Villanueva, writing an introductory blurb for Section Four of *Cross-Talk in Comp Theory* (1997), also argues, implicitly, that we need to look below the surface of scientistic or positivistic claims in order to see the hidden, socially constructed assumptions informing them. He has this to say about scientism: "Scientism or positivism, then is inherently flawed, since in claiming to transcend the 'social and political,' it fails to make explicit (or even recognize) the effects of the social in its inquiries" (391). I agree with Gleason and Villanueva and others who look for and find evidence of writers' apparent assumptions embedded in the language structures they use. I do it, too. My point here, with which I'm sure Gleason and Villanueva would agree, is that the analyzers are analyzing others' assumptions through their own assumption-colored haze, which is much harder to see because it is never not there.

Granted, those engaged in empirical research may not be sufficiently conscious of the ways in which what they "observe" is constructed by forces outside their laboratories. The research is then flawed, but so is the compunction in our field to discard anything that comes out of a mode of inquiry not primarily emphasizing the primacy of language and its link with the social constructedness of knowledge. The almost total rejection of empirically based research by top theorists in Composition suggests a capitulation to binarism that is surprising.

Perhaps our love of words is a larger part of our epistemological base than we are willing to acknowledge, even to ourselves. We like to interpret and reinterpret other people's words. We interpret their interpretations, and we try to interpret our own. To use Ann E. Berthoff's phrase—who used I. A. Richard's—we examine the meaning of our meanings.[7]

Not only do we love to interpret whole texts; we love individual words, too—special words that we make up, or that other people have used before and reuse, re-define, or re-shape for our own purposes, running it through our own text. Patricia Bizzell has commented on our proclivity for singling out a special word or "resonant phrase" that "will become current in the disciplinary discourse precisely because it is morally ambiguous." In her "Afterword" to *Academic Discourse and Critical Consciousness*, she points to "critical consciousness" as such an example (1992, 231).

We also take our special words and show how they can be used in a new way. I did so in this chapter when I used Greg Myers' definition of *ideology* to say something about Composition's privileging of writing. In his book *Defending Access*, Tom Fox (1999) borrows Barbara Herrnstein Smith's use of the word *contingencies* (4). John Trimbur uses Roland Barthes' *acratic discourse* (1989, 608). Carol Berkenkotter and

Thomas Huckin, in their conclusion to a study cited in the last footnote, use Bakhtin's word, *centripetalization* (1995, 116).

We privilege those we do for their theories, their studies, or their scholarship. But we also privilege them for their turns of phrase. The leftover poet in us, the remnant of our past and/or current love of belles lettres, loves to quote Britton's "shaping at the point of utterance," Freire's "banking concept of education," Berthoff's "making of meaning," Elbow's "believing and doubting game," North's "making of knowledge," Burke's "parlor," and Bruffee's "conversation of mankind," who in turn is quoting Michael Oakeshott. And so it goes.

Although we may not acknowledge our dependence on words *as words*, on their place in our worldview and rhetorical strategies, it is clear that in Composition our way of knowing privileges written words, interpretation of words, made-up words, recovery of old words, word play, and clever word combinations. There is nothing wrong with this. But this playing in the sandbox with colorful words is not what everyone likes to do.

As feminist theory has taught us, it is much easier to see someone else's ideology than it is to see one's own. We can't step outside our own lens. But we can at least admit we have this worship of the written word and notion of writing as the most accurate indicator of learning. Examining our own investedness in the writing-as-the-great-heuristic ideology might help us realize what harm a reverence for written language might have on students who do not share our love for words and allow us to recognize alternatives to alphabetic-based ways of knowing.

It might be productively depressing to admit we are players in what Berkenkotter calls "a paradigm debate" or "a turf war" (I like special phrases, too) about whose research agendas and epistemological assumptions are the most sophisticated or radical. Such ideological disagreements can look a lot like a schoolyard fight about whose parent has the best job, a tiresome binary typical of hegemonic Western culture. Such battles, with their underlying assumptions about right and wrong, winners and losers, are really unarticulated acceptances of the Platonic view that there is a "right" or "true" way of doing things.[8] We may have to come to terms with the possibility that as writing instructors and people whose lives revolve around written words, we may be trying (albeit with all good intentions) to foist upon our students a way of thinking that we prefer.

Writing and its role in thinking does not have to be conceived of as a binary. We can still believe in the primacy of language even as we hold it suspect. We can respect other signs of intellectual insight even as we self-consciously promote writing as our area of expertise. With our students, we can play with different instruments, juggle different tools, experiment with how different worldviews and intellectual pathways

might complicate and enrich each other. We might see different epistemologies not as hierarchical opposites but as adjacent possibilities about
how people make knowledge. But if they are "contraries," let us "embrace" them, as Peter Elbow advises, for the dialectic they provide and
the rethinking they make us do.

Finding Lost Threads in Composition Theory

The problem is, with the disciplinary focus on writing as knowing,
Composition allowed vital influences to disappear from its theory-base.
Over and over, we quote particular theorists who have an established
ethos in our field, and we cite the movements they began. However, we
often foreground only that part of their theory or practice that fits
what we're trying to show about the importance of writing and its
constructedness.

The Writing Across the Curriculum (WAC) movement is a case in
point. As David R. Russell, Nancy Martin, Robert Parker, Vera Goodkin,
Dan Mahala, and others have pointed out, our *writing* across the curriculum programs were influenced by Britain's earlier movement, which
focused not on improving writing per se, but on learning. The current
foundering of many WAC programs may be due to institutions' mis-
understanding of the original British model's radical view of the role
language plays in thinking—all forms of language, formal and expres-
sive writing, classroom talk and dialogue, as well as dramatics.[9] In the
British education reform movement of the 1960s, James Britton, Nancy
Martin, and others used writing as a way of promoting learning across
the curriculum, but they also used children's everyday spoken language as well as other forms of activity-as-learning. Nancy Martin especially was influenced by play and its role in intellectual development.
However, when the *language* across the curriculum theories and practices Britton and Martin and others promoted in Britain came to the
United States, they were reconfigured as *writing* across the curriculum
programs, often promoted by reformers—and accepted by administrators—as ways to help students improve their writing—lamentations
about the poor quality of which are both old and ubiquitous (see Chapter 6). Instead of understanding the whole theoretical base informing
the British reform movement, and the variety of practices used in it,
Composition professionals here foregrounded the intellectual work of
their favorite heuristic—writing—and, with a few exceptions, let the
other modes of learning fall away.[10]

In his 1985 essay that won the Braddock award, Peter Elbow argued that we should explore more thoroughly the intersections of

speech and writing in our teaching, that we should take advantage of both the "indelible" and "ephemeral" aspects of writing and the immediate, dramatic elements of speech, for what they can offer in support of writing pedagogy (283–303). However, Elbow is mostly cited for his promotion of freewriting and ways of responding.

Another theorist whose comprehensive work has been appropriated in ways that privilege only one part of it is Janet Emig. As I have pointed out elsewhere, in Emig's 1978 article, "Hand, Eye, Brain," she called for Composition to work more closely with biology departments to find out what their research might contribute to knowledge about writing development (70). However, as David R. Russell and Patricia Bizzell have shown, it was Emig's "Writing as a Mode of Learning" that was highly influential in promoting the idea of writing as a unique mode of learning. This piece became a cornerstone of the writing-as-primary-heuristic ideological structure of the field. As is obvious, Emig's advice to Compositionists in "Hand, Eye, Brain" to collaborate on research with biologists was left behind. What the field did carry around on its shoulders, however, was her argument in "Writing as a Mode of Learning" that *writing*—specifically writing, not speech—is a unique and powerful intellectual tool.

In that oft-quoted article, Emig opposed the use of speech mostly because it could not be easily recorded and transcribed: "Talking is creating *and* originating a verbal construct that is *not* graphically recorded (except for the circuitous routing of a transcribed tape)" (her emphasis 1977, 123). This was an objection to speech that Nancy Sommers also voiced: "The possibility of revision distinguishes the written text from speech" (1980, 379). Until very recently, there were practical reasons to work more with written language than with speech. Writing could be analyzed and revised. Speech could not, unless it were recorded and then transcribed, a painfully slow process.

However, Emig's (1977) and Sommers' (1980) objection to speech has been ameliorated by twenty-first-century voice-type dictation computer technologies. First there was discrete speech voice recognition: a computer could transcribe human speech, but not very accurately, and—the—words—had—to—be—separated—and—spoken—quite —mechanically—like—this. By 1997, however, natural-voice recognition programs became available, though each user had to read a fairly lengthy text to the computer in order to "train" the program to recognize the user's individual voice and accent. At the 2000 CCCC in Minneapolis, Charles Lowe pointed out (at the only presentation I could find on voice-recognition technology, by the way) that now a mere five-minute prep time could prepare a natural-voice recognition word processor to understand a speaker (writer).

Now, twenty years after Emig's celebration of writing for its ease of being accessed and analyzed, speech-to-text technology makes "speaking" look more like "writing." As Lowe points out, speech-to-text on screen is much like freewriting on screen: both potential first-draft material that can be developed, manipulated, revised, or discarded. What Emig and Sommers objected to regarding the limits of speech is no longer true, at least for those with access to voice-recognition technology (access to technology in general being another issue related to privilege which Cynthia Selfe has addressed). But Lowe also argues that speaking may involve different intellectual processes than writing, especially for people used to creating text through their fingertips. These processes have not been studied in Composition, Lowe points out. In a recent issue of the online journal *Kairos*, Stanley Harrison (2000) is even more alarmed at Composition's lack of interest in automated speech recognition (ASR) technologies. He points out business interests have already seized upon ASR and says that Composition's failure to theorize this substantial technological breakthrough may render us powerless to affect its cultural work "in service to the dominant order." He warns,

> Indeed, by the time that ASR word processing programs become an integral component of computer-assisted freshman and basic writing classes, compositionists may find it difficult to conceive of ASR except in terms of its relationship to business communication. (1)

While I don't disagree with Harrison, I submit that our failure to take up and theorize voice-to-text breakthroughs may be due to our field's privileging of, and our own proclivities toward, *writing*.

The reception in our field of Lev S. Vygotksy's work is another example of how we root around in someone else's work, pulling out for our use only what fits our epistemological frame. Fortunately, there are several notable exceptions. Informed introductions to Vygotsky outline the breadth of his work. They discuss his emphasis on tools and play in learning as well as on the role of the social. Alex Kozulin, in his introduction to his edition of *Thought and Language*, foregrounds both aspects of Vygotsky's work: "According to Vygotsky, human higher mental functions must be viewed as products of *mediated* activity. The role of mediator is played by *psychological tools* and means of interpersonal communication" (his emphasis, 1989, xxiv). Similarly, in their essay "Exploring Vygotskian Perspectives in Education," Ellice A. Forman and Courtney B. Cazden write in their first sentence: "Two important and related themes in Vygotsky's writings are the social foundations of cognition and the importance of instruction in development" (in Wertsch 1989, 323). And in their separate and comprehensive interpretations of

Vygotsky, both Myra Barrs (1988, 52) and James Zebroski (1994, 198) have argued that writing begins in movement, gesture, and play.

However, other citations of Vygotsky seem to use him primarily to support the social nature of learning. It's not that they argue with Vygotsky's emphasis on tools, play, and hands-on activity. It's that Vygotsky seems synonymous with emphasis on the social, an authority to cite to support the writer's argument for the role of the social in language and learning.

In their Afterword to *Mind in Society*, for example, Vera John-Steiner and Ellen Souberman recognize Vygotsky's "emphasis upon an active organism" (1978, 123). They immediately follow that statement, however, with what they seem to view as his more important contribution: "While Piaget stresses biologically supported, universal stages of development, Vygotsky's emphasis is on the interaction between changing social conditions and the biological substrata of behavior" (123). John-Steiner and Souberman give an eloquent and complete view of Vygotsky's contributions. In their concluding paragraph, they list all the areas Vygotsky influenced: "The impact of Vygotsky's work— as that of great theoreticians everywhere—is both general and specific. Cognitive psychologists as well as educators are interested in exploring the present-day implications of his notions, whether they refer to play, to the genesis of scientific concepts, or to the relation of thought and language" (133). Even they, however, whose overview of Vygotsky is one of the more balanced ones available, reveal what they view as his most important contribution:

> Perhaps the most distinguishing theme of Vygotsky's writing is his emphasis on the unique qualities of our species, how as human beings we actively realize and change ourselves in the varied contexts of culture and history. (131)

Compositionists seem more interested in Vygotsky's emphasis on language and social interaction than they are in his work on the role emotions, and hands-on activity play in learning. To use a bad analogy, it's like Vygotsky was flying a number of flags, but Compositionists run only one up the pole: the emphasis on the social. Here is Mark Wiley in his introduction to the "Political Key" section of the *Composition in Four Keys* (1996) collection explaining Vygotsky's influence. Wiley foregrounds the "social materialist" aspect of Vygotsky's work. He doesn't argue with Vygotsky's related theories on tools and play; he just doesn't mention them:

> The emphasis on the social nature of language led scholars to examine the material sources for our thinking. This social materialist orientation toward cognition gathered momentum through the influence

of Lev Vygotsky's theories concerning the place of "mind in society." Vygotsky postulated that all higher mental activity originates in the social sphere. The fact that Vygotsky's thinking arose within a Marxist context (whether scholars wanted to recognize this fact or not) directed attention toward the relation between individual thought and larger social and ideological systems within which our thinking is embedded. (419)

Linda Shaw Finlay and Valerie Faith explain in the introduction to their essay in *Freire for the Classroom* how they draw from both Freire and Vygotsky. They discuss Vygotsky's theories regarding inner speech and its relation to writing. But then they collapse both Freire and Vygotsky in a way that serves to emphasize only one aspect of each. Their summary of what both Freire and Vygotsky contribute is valid, but their characterization of what both "emphasize" makes it easy for future citers of Freire and Vygotsky to foreground what each said about social relations and society, and to forget what Freire said about "multiple channels" (to be discussed in the next chapter) and what Vygotsky said about active play. This perfectly fine summary is significant for what it omits:

> Freire's pedagogy, which respects the connection between the critical use of language and an awareness of oneself in social relations, dovetails with Vygotsky's developmental psychology. Both emphasize the importance of the interaction between persons and cultural elements in moving from inner speech to written language. So, relying on Freire and Vygotsky, we decided to approach language teaching through our students' understanding of the relationship between language and society, between the use of words and the structure of their reality. (64)

This condensed view and selected privileging of the theories of Freire, Vygotsky, Emig, Britton, Martin, and others is typical of what we in Composition do because of our ideological beliefs about words. We sift theories for what appeals to us, and we leave behind what they did with other ways of knowing. As James Porter, Patricia Sullivan, Stuart Blythe, Jeffrey T. Grabill, and Libby Miles point out in a recent *CCC* article, as much as Foucault is cited in our field, "the visual and spatial aspects of his work are largely undervalued" (634). We have danced with the verbal and the social construction. We have left as wallflowers the role emotion, confidence, movement, visualization, and sometimes even oral language, play in learning.

One extended example of how Composition has promoted *writing* as an almost exclusive way of knowing is to examine Paulo Freire's reception in our field, especially how only select portions of Freire's praxis have been privileged in our discussions of him. Our treatment of Freire's work is such an illustrative example; the next chapter is devoted to it.

Notes

1. See John S. Mayher's (1990) book *Uncommon Sense: Theoretical Practice in Language Education*, Portsmouth, NH: Boynton/Cook Heinemann, for insightful observations on how "commonsense" attitudes have prevented schools from making meaningful reforms. I address this issue further in Chapter 6.

2. Kutz and Roskelly are right that teachers should also "Consider the implications of gender, class, race, and ethnicity in making assignments, in creating classroom dynamics of groups. And consider the effect of stereotypes in deciding about abilities potential" (115). However, they do not specifically acknowledge different learning styles, talents, or intelligences.

3. As Alex Kozulin points out, Vygotsky was "an aspiring literary critic" (xiii). Michael Cole and Sylvia Scribner point out in their Introduction to *Mind in Society*, that Vygotsky "made several contributions to literary criticism" (1). In their biographical sketch of his life, they note that Vygotsky taught literature as well as psychology (15).

4. *People Weekly*, June 19, 2000, p. 48.

5. See the discussion of Gerald Coles and others in Chapter 1 of my book, *Learning Re-Abled* (1995).

6. In a footnote in his anthologized essay in Buffington et al.'s *Living Languages*, Graff credits McLeod for pointing this out to him.

7. Our link with word-loving literary studies is also demonstrated in Carol Berkenkotter's and Thomas N. Huckin's analysis of a cross section of individual CCCC proposals from 1988, 1989, 1990, and 1992. In their description of the 1988 and 1989 proposals, they noted that "the field seems, in recent years, to be moving increasingly toward a more hermeneutical mode of inquiry by adopting from literary studies the activity of problematization" (107). Their 1992 sampling of high-rated proposals, however, showed more empirical studies. They explain in a footnote that since the CCCC Executive Council barred research on proposal abstracts, 1992 was the last year they were able to study. Based on the trends and changes they saw from 1988–1992, however, they conclude that the field seems to be moving toward "generic blends," which include a mix of categories: empirical, practice, and hermeneutic (114). Based on my own experience of reading proposals for the last three years and attending every CCCC conference for the last ten years, I think the trend is moving back towards the hermeneutic, but I have not investigated paper titles systematically.

8. I am indebted to Ken Lindblom for this idea regarding Platonism.

9. For a more complete discussion of this point, see my "Forgotten Elements in Writing Across the Curriculum," in *Issues in Writing* 9.1 (Fall/Winter 1998): 19–42.

10. Another reason writing, and not speaking, is emphasized in Composition Studies is explained by Diana George and John Trimbur in their account of the composition/communication split that occurred in the early days of CCCC history. They point out that the February 1960 issue of *CCC* published a report on future directions for CCCC. Besides recommending a focus on first-year writing and on composition as a discipline, the report pointed to the goal of improving "college students' understanding and use of the English language, *especially in written discourse*" (George and Trimbur's emphasis, 1990. *CCC* 50(4): [June] 691). They also point out the irony that when "the communication battle" was over, and writing had triumphed over other forms of communication, Ken Macrorie, as *CCC* editor, introduced to the 1963 issue the logo of the sunburst, using "the tools of sign-making and graphic design to consolidate the victory of the word over image" (693).

Chapter Two

Paulo Freire's "Multiple Channels of Communication"

Only those who have power can decide what constitutes intellectualism.[1]

—Paulo Freire

One way to understand why Composition has promoted *writing* as an almost exclusive way of knowing is to examine Paulo Freire's reception in our field, especially how only select portions of Freire's praxis have been privileged in our discussions of him. In the United States, applications of Paulo Freire's liberatory teaching have, for the most part, emphasized his problematizing approach, his "desocialization" of students. He helps students become critically conscious of their position in the larger socioeconomic condition so that they can become subjects, rather than objects, of their education, and so they have the potential to name and transform the world.

Compositionists seem less aware or less interested in Freire's insistence on what he called "the use of multiple channels of communication" (1993, 49), which took advantage of different people's aural, spatial, visual, and kinesthetic ways of knowing to help them problematize the "codifications" in his culture circles (42–45).

Since the people with whom Freire was working were illiterate, he had to rely at least initially on visual images, oral discussions, and other non-written modes. These alternate pathways, however, invited learner participation. They allowed people to succeed using a format with which they had confidence. Not only did these techniques develop students' political consciousness, they also explicitly and implicitly acknowledged and supported multiple ways of knowing. He used these in his radical teaching to challenge traditional linguistic-based primers, as well as their conventional assumptions regarding word-based knowledge making.

The "multiple channel" aspect of his praxis has not been fore-grounded in Composition perhaps because we are unreflective of our own investment in, and privileging of, the word-based teaching prac-tices discussed in the last chapter, even some that purport to be adap-tations of Freire's conscientization. Even as we promote the dialectical problematizing of other socially constructed assumptions, we seem unaware of our own overuse of one channel of communication—writ-ing—as a way of knowing.

Examining Paulo Freire's status in our field will provide a lens through which we can study Composition's focus on social issues as subject, as well as on the over-dependence on written words as heuris-tics. The story of what we have done with Freire's work parallels the story of what we have done with other people's work (Britton, Martin, Vygotsky, Emig), whose inclusive theories about learning have been appropriated to support a limited view of language, and to discourage alternate symbol systems. By shifting the focus to equally important aspects of Freire's praxis, ones that have not been taken up with the same zeal, I want to argue that an especially important social injustice Freire addressed, which many of his imitators have not, is the socially constructed privileging of writing as a way of knowing.

The following discussion of Freire is not presented in binary oppo-sition to other interpretations, but rather as a supplement to them. In fact, part of my argument is a critique of critiques and false oppositions, and a plea for nuanced "both/and" theorizing, which can tolerate "con-tradictions." Contradictions, after all, force the dialectical inquiry cru-cial to the critical theory most of us claim to promote.[2]

Freire not only melded theory and practice in a way that is not done enough even among his most ardent supporters, and hardly at all in the academy. He studied thinking processes and privileged intellec-tual pathways that went beyond written, even beyond oral-based, ways of knowing. He theorized them and practiced them. And then, because self-reflection was a basic tenet of his praxis, he retheorized his ap-proach, using self-critique in a way that kept him open to change. His interdisciplinary background, also rare in our discipline-strict academy, made him aware of, and curious about, a wide variety of philosophical, epistemological, and linguistic theories that informed, and then rein-formed, his self-reflective praxis. By revisiting Freire's tapestry of work, by examining different threads, we can ask different questions about the frame of our own assumptions.

Freire's Reception

I didn't invent a method, or a theory, or a program, or a system, or a pedagogy,
or a philosophy. It is people who put names to things.

—Paulo Freire[3]

In the last thirty years, Paulo Freire's work with illiterate adults in Brazil
and Chile has been praised, modeled, analyzed, and critiqued in books,
essays, and articles too numerous to recount, and only a fraction of
which appear in the Works Cited section of this book. Following his
death in 1997, there were a number of commemorative books and
journal volumes: one in *JAC: A Journal of Composition Theory;* two issues
of *Convergence* (1998); two 1999 Boynton/Cook collections of essays,
edited by Ira Shor and Caroline Pari, on using Freirean principles in
teaching (*Education Is Politics: Critical Teaching Across Differences, K–12,* and
Critical Literacy in Action: Writing Words, Changing Worlds), and a number
of websites devoted to Freire and his work. As Rosa-María Torres points
out, 30,000 copies of Freire's last book, *Pedagogy of Autonomy* (1997)
"sold out in a few days" (111).

Why, in the twenty-first century, should we study Freire's praxis?
One reason is that his illiterate students learned very quickly. Freire
pointed out that in less than two months, people who previously could
not read would be "writing notes and simple letters and discussing
problems of local and national interest" (1993, 53). His work has influenced and inspired thousands of teachers all over the world. As Torres
writes in the tribute issue of *Convergence:*

> Paulo, the great communicator, the great inspirer, helped millions of
> people discover and bring to the surface the best in themselves: their
> human, generous, compassionate side; the inner drive to become a
> volunteer, an inventor, a hero, a revolutionary. (114)

Because of Freire's success, many have attempted to adapt selected
aspects of his teaching. And these adaptations have themselves been
criticized, as has Freire's work itself. In foregrounding Freire's attention
to "multiple channels of communication," I risk the judgment that I
am appropriating his ideas, misrepresenting his purposes, or ignoring
his critique of what he called "the capitalist production mode" (Torres
1998, 109).[4] Part of our culture's language/thought frame is both a
dichotomy and a hierarchy, with an inescapable logic that goes like this:
"This is a privileging of Freire's use of multiple channels. It must therefore ignore his overall cultural critique." I am guilty of a similarly di-
chotomous thought when I critique those who focus on Freire's cultural
critique but do not foreground his multisensory teaching. However,
Freire's use of multi-modal approaches was *also* a demonstrated cultural critique. Even those who have focused on his "method," or those
who have condemned others' focus on "method," have not stressed the

importance of Freire's theorized decision to use these approaches as a concomitant representation of his theory.

Educators in the United States have had only limited success with trying to "import" what Freire did, because as Freire points out, people often do not reinvent his approaches, only copy them. Since copying does not involve the rethinking, dialectic, and self-reflectiveness with which Freire reinvented his own work, Freirean imitators who do not self-critique are not adopting what may be the most crucial aspect of Freire's work. As Freire put it, "In order to follow me, it is essential not to follow me."[5]

What Freire did first was study the students themselves and to listen to them. Such a study would discover that the context for teaching—the students, the teachers, the circumstances, everything—is different from what Freire encountered and would therefore have to be reinvented. Therefore, any pedagogy is doomed that does not look at students anew. Besides failing to reinvent their own practice, "Freirian tourists" [his phrase, 1997, 308] have focused on problem-posing, and even occasionally on oral problem-posing, but that's not enough. They have especially ignored the multi-dimensional nature of Freire's work.

Many educators are familiar with Freire's critique of "the banking model" of education, which exposed the undemocratic assumptions supporting oppressive literacy programs and the societies that produced them. Many also use discussion to promote critical consciousness. They seem less aware of Freire's emphasis on an educational process that "requires multiple techniques to achieve a particular goal" (1997, 304–305). While there are many reasons to keep Freire's work at the center of any serious literacy reform, the one that interests me here is one that has been undertheorized: his use of what he called "the use of multiple channels of communication" (1993, 49).

The Multiple Channels

Freire's praxis depended on these multiple channels and techniques, which may have greatly influenced his students' success in ways that have not been fully realized in thirty years of Freirean adaptations. He used these in his radical teaching to challenge traditional linguistic-based primers as well as their users' tacit assumptions regarding knowledge making. Freire used multi-dimensional representations or "channels of communication" to help students gain perspective on "existential situations": pictures, slides, or large posters; "group debate"; "oral synthesis"; dialogue, songs, or physical objects themselves (1993, 42–54). While Freire's promotion of critical consciousness was radical and liberating, his radical and liberating pedagogy itself demonstrated critique. His techniques were not add-ons, not situated below theory, as they often are in academia today. Freire's techniques and Freire's social activism were of a piece.

However, Freire's techniques, especially the multi-dimensional nature of them, have been undertheorized. Overall, as Paul Taylor has observed, "little attention has actually been given to the Culture Circles and the content of Freire's method."[6] Taylor asks, "If Freire's method actually works, why does it work?" (1993, 82). And Henry Giroux, in his Introduction to *Literacy: Reading the Word and the World,* argues that "the relevance of the notion of pedagogy as part of a critical theory of education is either undertheorized or merely forgotten" (Freire 1987, 18).

Perhaps because of his varied interests and interdisciplinary background (see Taylor and Elias), Freire had a deep interest in "the way they [the people] construct their thought" (1973,103). Over and over, Freire emphasized that *how* people made meaning should be respected: "For the notion of literacy to become meaningful it has to be situated within a theory of cultural production and *viewed as an integral part of the way in which people produce, transform, and reproduce meaning"* (my emphasis, 1993, 142).

Freire had a "both/and" view of theory and practice. For example, problem-posing, dialogic approaches foster critical consciousness *and* provide what Freire called the "active educational method [that] helps a person become consciously aware of his [or her] context and his condition as a human being as Subject . . . " (1993, 56). Not only do the "existential situations" Freire used in his classes develop students' political consciousness, they also explicitly and implicitly acknowledge and support multiple ways of knowing. While Compositionists should continue to privilege the critical consciousing so important to Freire's praxis, we should also problematize our own print-dependent, and possibly oppressive, classroom activities.

Freire's Response to Critique

In his response to critiques of his work, and to claims that pedagogies purporting to be Freirean-based are not always successful in North America, Freire says that the "written form" has been "bureaucratized" in North American schools:

> This is a fundamental way in which schools in North America maintain and expand an antidemocratic system—through distancing students from a frozen written word and therefore discouraging them from thinking of themselves as actors in history. Language is first and

foremost oral. We don't begin with writing. History did not begin in a written form, but in words and actions. (1997, 323)

For Freire, who was both a reformer and a teacher, epistemology was as crucial as literacy. How did pople come to know? How could he engage the students? Unlike many theorists today, Freire did focus on teaching itself, especially on how to work with and develop what students could already do: "Thus what challenges me is not so much how to facilitate the reading of various sounds of the language; but *how to develop the capacity that human beings have to know*" (my emphasis, 1997, 305).

Freire believed strongly in the role talk and dialogue play in coming to know. In her tribute to Freire, Ann Berthoff points out that "'the pedagogy of knowing' is Freire's phrase, not mine, and that without that idea, 'the pedagogy of the oppressed' is a sterile slogan" (1997, 308). In a chapter he wrote with Donaldo Macedo, "Adult Literacy and Popular Libraries," Freire called for public libraries to be more than "a silent depository of books . . ." (45). He recommended that older residents of rural areas, as well as artisans and poets, be interviewed on tape, their stories becoming just as much a part of library resources as are books.

This respect for the oral was also reflected in the way he chose to present his views. He used talk and dialectic even in his published texts. As Paul Taylor points out (1993, 31), Freire composed three "talked books": *A Pedagogy for Liberation: Dialogues on Transforming Education* (1987); *Literacy: Reading the Word and the World* (1987); and *Learning to Question: A Pedagogy of Liberation* (1989). Taylor says these talked books are an opportunity for Freire "to repeat his view that literacy acquisition should be in the natural language of the people and not in the dominant language of the educator or of the cultural invader" (32).

These transcriptions of dialogue also demonstrate Freire's endorsement of the dialogic. Even in books that are not reproductions of live dialogue, the importance of dialogue is evident. In *Mentoring the Mentor: A Critical Dialogue with Paulo Freire*, Freire responds in the final chapter to issues raised in fifteen previous chapters by a variety of teacher/scholars. He talks about the importance of orality and dialogue as heuristics, as ways of *coming to know*. It is worth quoting at length here because in addressing complaints that his methods do not "work" in the United States, Freire critiques what he see as an overemphasis on writing as the primary tool used in teaching:

> For example, when Donaldo Macedo and I are talking in a dialogue we both become more creative. In part this is because of our background as oral individuals who were not socialized in the written text only. What would be really interesting and important is if a society,

through school, when reaching the graphic moment—the written form—would not turn it so as to bureaucratize it. In other words, when society which is by nature oral, reaches the written stage, it should not freeze orality by bureaucratizing it. Orality requires solidarity with the Other. Orality is dialogical by its very nature to the extent that you cannot do it individualistically. Thus the challenge for schools is not to kill those values of solidarity that lead to democratic space through a process that freezes the required dialogical nature of orality through the individualistic apprehension of reading and writing. This is really fundamental. *Students who are extremely conversant in orality must therefore never be reduced to one form of thinking that is linear and individualistic. Ironically, schools do this all the time, reducing students to a nonoral and linear form of reading and thinking.* (my emphasis, 1997, 322–23)

Freire deliberately worked with dialogue, even in his published texts, in order to foreground the importance of talk and of oral, dynamic, ongoing challenge to ideas. The live dialectic demonstrates Freire's theory: "The text of this conversation is an example of how we think in all of these dimensions" (329).

"Tactical, Technical, Methodological Ways"

Freire experimented with these different dimensions and urged teachers to look beyond conventional pedagogies and to realize that a teacher's language can intimidate and silence students. Teachers should acknowledge this power, Freire says, and should therefore cultivate ways of listening to students' "silenced voices." Then, teachers could "begin to look for ways—*tactical, technical, methodological ways*—that could facilitate the process of reading the silenced word that is in a close relationship with the lived world of the students" (my emphasis, 1997, 306–307).

Freire used "tactical, technical, methodological ways" in his teaching. Several accounts of Freire's pedagogy print the ten "codifications" or "visual representations" of life in the peasants' world. These visualizations sparked discussions and dialogue, tapping into and developing students' visual and oral literacies. However, as Deborah Barndt has pointed out, Freire's codifications were not limited to the pictures and slides. They involved "photographs, slides, posters, reading texts, newspapers, recorded interviews, dramatizations, etc." (63). In her teaching in Lima, Peru and Toronto, Canada, Barndt uses sociodramas, cartoons, music, soap operas, photo-novels, and three-dimensional objects (such as tomatoes) as codes most appropriate to the cultural roots of her students.

As Freire explains in *Pedagogy of the Oppressed,* the codifications could take many forms, or what Freire called "channels"—the visual, tactile, auditive, or they could be combinations of channels, which he called "compound codifications":

> Once the breakdown of the thematics is complete, there follows the stage of its "codification": *choosing the best channel of communication* for each theme and its representation. A codification may be simple or compound. The former utilizes *either the visual (pictoral or graphic), the tactile, or the auditive channel; the latter utilizes various channels.* The selection of the pictoral or graphic channel depends not only on the material to be codified, but also on whether or not the individuals with whom one wishes to communicate are literate. (my emphasis, 1973, 114–15)

Always the teacher who uses multiple pathways even to explain the need for multiple pathways, Freire follows the above prose explanation with an outline in footnote 38 at the bottom of the page:

[38] CODIFICATION
  a) Simple:
        visual channel
              pictoral
              graphic
        tactile channel
        auditive channel
  b) Compound: simultaneity of channels. (115)

Again and again, however, these alternate inroads to thinking are not highlighted in discussions of Freire's work.

Cultural Work Outside and Inside the Classroom

With some exceptions, those teacher/scholars who cite Freire as an influence emphasize his promotion of critical consciousness. Or they begin by describing his practice, only to imply its secondary position focusing on what they view as the more important cultural work to be done *outside* the classroom. Those who do call for more attention to his practice mostly stress only one aspect of it: the use of the oral discussions in the Culture Circles.

A few teacher/scholars (e.g., Nan Alsasser and Vera John-Steiner, Ira Shor, Nancy Schneidewind, Nina Wallerstein) have seriously addressed the partipatory and fully interactive approaches called for in Freire's work. These "multiple channels" tap into the aural, spatial, visual, and kinesthetic ways of knowing used by different people.[7]

In their adaptation of Freirean codification, Nina Wallerstein and Edward Bernstein have their students conduct on-site interviews with hospital patients and jail residents. Then the students produce other multisensory codes—songs, slides, collages, and videos—to promote dialogue about the social issues the patients and inmates must contend with: alcoholism, substance abuse, and low wages (60). In their summary of what they call Freire's "three-stage methodology," however, Wallerstein and Bernstein emphasize "listening," "participatory dialogue," and "action or positive change." They do not draw attention to the multi-dimentional nature of the students' work.

Freire's attention to demonstrated theory, his respect for practice, especially multi-dimensional practice, exceeds that of some of his most ardent supporters. In spite of Freire's "both/and" philosophy of *praxis,* a word that fuses theory and practice, some of Freire's promoters seem to reveal an "either/or" conception of them. They privilege his theory, foregrounding the non-traditional subject matter and beyond-the-classroom social activism inherent in Freire's praxis. Even those who begin by pointing to Freire's blending of theory and practice soon complain that Freire's work has been "reduced" to discussions of practice, technique, and method. Like the same poles of a magnet, theory and practice cannot seem be placed next to each other for long as equals in academic writing. They repel and realign every time, into a hierarchy, with theory always on top.

The Theory/Practice Hierarchy

This troublesome separation of theory and practice in the academy, especially the reverence for theory and dismissal of practice, shows itself in the most unexpected places. More than most teacher/scholars, Ira Shor has stressed the importance of Freire's classroom practice. In an essay called "Education Is Politics," Shor argues that a crucial part of "a Freirean class" involves attention to "the learning process itself" (in McLaren and Leonard 1993, 25). He reminds us that "Freire insists on consistency between the democratic values of this critical pedagogy and its classroom practices" (27). In fact, says Shor, *"the whole activity of education is political in nature"* (Shor's emphasis, 27). Inseparable from classroom practice, and inseparable from politics, as Shor points out, is "the punitive attitude of the curriculum towards everyday speech and non-standard English spoken by students" (27).

I agree with Shor, as he argues in *Freire for the Classroom,* that a "both/and" approach to solving inequalities is needed:

> Teacher burnout and student resistance are social problems of an unequal system and cannot be *fully* addressed by teacher-education reforms or by classroom remedies *alone.* Participatory and critical

> pedagogy coupled with egalitarian policies in school and society can
> *holistically* address the education crisis. (his emphases, 1987, 13)

Social inequalities outside the classroom do impact, in fact, *cause* many
social inequalities within the classroom (for example, the resources
available in rich school districts versus the lack of sufficient resources in
poor ones; access to technology in some schools and not in others; high
expectations of students in some schools and not in others, etc.).

Even Shor, however, who more than most scholars promotes attention to practice-as-politics, especially in his earlier work, seems in
his more recent writing to view practice as less important, after all, than
other social inequalities. In his early *Critical Teaching and Everyday Life*
(1980), Shor writes,

> We have little choice but to situate liberatory teaching in the anti-
> liberatory field conditioning of the classroom. This kind of project is
> no different from other exercises in social change, which begin from
> the concrete reality they are destined to negate. (269)

In his teaching, Shor uses concrete objects and a variety of multisensory strategies to problematize social conditions. In his early work
on Freire, Shor describes a number of approaches that use drama, mime,
"visual puzzles," grids, concentric circles, and of course his most famous concrete object—a real hamburger—to help students conceptualize abstract ideas. In his later work, however, although Shor continues to say that pedagogy is important, more and more he emphasizes
the theorizing of external social issues. Even as he celebrates pedagogy
in this early work, he seems to see it on a lower, or separate, rung, than
social concerns: "I have characterized learning as a broad social problem rather than as a narrow pedagogical or personal one" (269).

However, pedagogical problems are not always "narrow" and are
always already social. As I think Shor would agree, from the moment
a teacher walks into a classroom, her "practical method" already reveals itself as accepting or challenging conventional notions regarding
ways of knowing. The explicit or implicit belief that facility with *written*
language is the most important indicator of sophisticated thinking is
itself a hegemonic assumption that results in unequal treatment of
people, especially in classrooms, where that belief dictates conventional
text-based practices. *At the same time* we problematize issues external
to the classroom, we should problematize issues *within* the classroom
regarding who is being oppressed—and whose interests are being
served—by unproblematized practical methods that are almost completely print-based.

Another example of this subtle separation of intention and method
appears in Shor's Preface to *Education Is Politics* ("The River of Reform").
Here he recommends a "bottom-up" reform that "contains multicul-

tural voices speaking for social justice and alternative methods" (vii). Many issues of social justice, of course, reside outside the immediate classroom environment, as Shor seems to imply by separating the phrases "social justice" *and* "alternative methods." However, using radically alternative methods in the class does more than speak for social justice. Using all ways of knowing, not just written-language-based ones, promotes and enacts a challenge to social injustices in the schoolroom so ingrained that even the best intentioned teacher/scholars may not see them.

In his later writings, when Shor discusses Freire's participatory classroom, he emphasizes student talk and student writing, not the other channels of communication Freire and his students used. Nor does he emphasize the harm done by written-word-based pedagogies to students whose primary ways of knowing are spatial, aural, or kinesthetic. In Shor's description of critical consciousness, he argues that Freirean desocialization would challenge society's myths that promote "racism, sexism, class bias, homophobia, a fascination with the rich and powerful, hero-worship, excess consumerism, runaway individualism, militarism, and national chauvinism" (McLaren and Leonard 1993, 32–33). Not mentioned are those who make knowledge in ways unfamiliar to their English or writing teachers. In Shor's list of Freirean pedagogical values, he says that a multicultural pedagogy would recognize "the various racial, ethnic, regional, age-based, and sexual cultures in society." Such teaching would be "balanced for gender, race, and class" (34). Not mentioned even in this otherwise comprehensive view of society's prejudices is the bias society has regarding ways of knowing. Word-based teaching is the dominant one in school cultures. Further, it may be that graphic, spatial, aural, kinesthetic, or other ways of knowing are especially under-used in writing classes because of the ways of knowing preferred by those who teach those classes.

I focus here on Shor because it is he who says the most about challenging conventional assumptions. He says the most about Freire's pedagogy emphasizing student writing and student talk. However, even Shor's comprehensive description of Freire's pedagogical values does not stress Freire's respect for learning in ways other than using words. If even Shor can leave that bias off his lists, what does that suggest about the teaching practices of those less sensitive to the power of deep-seated, unconscious cultural myths?

Oddly enough, even Henry Giroux may be inadvertently revealing an internalized dichotomy between theory and practice, and a privileging of theory over practice when he writes that Freire's work has been "appropriated by academic, adult educators, and others who inhabit the ideology of the West in ways that often reduce it to a pedagogical technique or method" (1993, 177). Given Giroux's promotion of the role of teaching in other writings, it is perhaps unfair to overly critique this decontextualized quotation. And he is no doubt correct that many people claim to be using a Freirean-influenced pedagogy simply because they pose questions to their students and allow discussions in their class. However, Giroux's use of the phrase "reduce it to a pedagogical technique or method," reveals that even one of pedagogy's most ardent supporters may harbor an estimation of method/technique that places it distinctly below "theory."

In "Paulo Freire's Radical Democratic Humanism," also in the McLaren and Leonard collection, Stanley Aronowitz also seems to at once separate theory and pedagogy, privileging the former and disrespecting the latter. He criticizes those who use and speak of Freire's work "as a 'teaching' method rather than a philosophical or social theory" (8). Granted, part of Aronowitz's point is that Freire's pedagogy was driven by his philosophy and social theory. However, the way "teaching method" is juxtaposed to "philosophical or social theory" suggests a disdain for "method," as do the scare quotes surrounding *teaching* but not *theory*.

In her Afterword to *Academic Discourse and Critical Consciousness*, Patricia Bizzell has commented on Composition's recent turn toward research and scholarship: "Now our professionalization has legitimated much research that has no immediate classroom application, . . ." (281). And Greg Myers candidly admits in "Reality, Consensus, and Reform, . . ." that even as he critiques the practices of Kenneth Bruffee, Peter Elbow, and Ken Macrorie, "I find I have no suggestions for assignments that are as innovative as those of the authors I am criticizing. But that is partly because what I have to suggest is not a method but a stance toward one's teaching" (169). While I agree with Myers that stance determines all else, it is disappointing that he does not consider "method" important enough to take a stab at putting his insightful critique into practice, of trying to design theoretically informed assignments or to describe what students actually do in his classes.

The Need for Confidence in Writing

Related to Freire's use of multiple, alternate routes to learning, is his sense that if people are to learn, if they are to connect with what is going on in the classroom, they must have confidence in themselves. Freire credits his first wife, Elza, whom Taylor says was a nursery school teacher who inspired Freire to become a teacher in the first place (19), with pointing out to him the role confidence plays in learning. In *Education for Critical Consciousness*, Freire relates how people who were illiterate one day were writing "words with complex phonemes" several days later. In a footnote explaining why this happened, Freire writes,

Interestingly enough, as a rule the illiterates wrote confidently and legibly, largely overcoming the natural indecisiveness of beginners. Elza Freire thinks this may be due to the fact that these persons, beginning with the discussion of the anthropological concept of culture, *discovered themselves to be more fully human, thereby acquiring an increasing emotional confidence in their learning which was reflected in their motor activity.* (my emphasis, 1993, 55)

While Elza Freire may have been right that the preceding discussion of culture may have helped the peasants see themselves as more "fully human," it may also be that by tapping into a variety of intellectual pathways—the visual, the aural, the kinesthetic—Freire was able to make all the people feel confident at least some of the time because at least some of the time each person's individual way of knowing was foregrounded. When the culture circle group worked with discovery cards, "the group (*not* the coordinator) begins to carry out oral synthesis" (Freire's emphasis, *Education for Critical Consciousness*, 55). No doubt those with good speaking skills shone during the frequent discussions. In a footnote describing his use of oral synthesis, Freire cites Gilson Amado's comment that "there is no such thing as oral illiteracy" (54). By using the oral debates to tap into what the students already knew, Freire helped them find confidence: "Many participants during these debates affirm happily and self-confidently that they are not being shown 'anything new, just remembering'" (47).

When the codification slides were projected, others may have been gifted at noticing things up on the screen. As Paul Taylor observes, there was a high level of "pictoral literacy" required to read some of the codifications (96). In her account of Freire's use of the pictures, Cynthia Brown points out that "By the time the group had reached this tenth picture, participants had regained enormous confidence in themselves, pride in their culture, and desire to learn to read" (225).

Early in my teaching career, I learned the importance confidence plays in student learning. My first teaching position was in a high school, where I taught both English and Driver Education. Instructing people to drive taught me a lot about teaching. Many of the students I taught were very hesitant, very scared beginners. They drove very, very slowly, and they took an excruciatingly long time sitting at stop signs, peering up and down the street for oncoming cars, and then peering up and down again just to make sure. By the time they actually moved their foot off the brake and placed it on the gas pedal, they—or usually I—would have to brake again because in the time they took to step on the gas, cars were now approaching.

I knew that if I didn't want to spend the rest of my life sitting at an intersection, I needed to find a way to help new drivers speed up their process of checking for traffic and accelerating. Stepping on the gas and moving into traffic requires a certain amount of confidence. Drivers need to make careful but quick decisions and then act on them. Beginning drivers do not respond well to picky criticism (as much as they might need it). And simply telling them to hurry up and pull out is not advice to give if one values one's own life. So I'd take raw beginners to safe areas where they could gradually build their skills and confidence. Wide, deserted streets in the suburbs. Big empty parking lots. Cemeteries. I let them get used to the feel of the gas pedal and the brake until they could start and stop smoothly, without giving the rest of us whiplash.

Instead of harping on what they were doing wrong ("Don't screech the brakes each time you stop. Don't keep alternating your right and left foot on the brake. Don't turn on the windshield wipers when you mean to signal right"), I'd try to find one small thing for which to praise them: "You're holding the steering wheel very nicely now." "You're looking up and down the street very thoroughly." "It's good you stopped completely for that stop sign." Gradually, I found I could validate more substantial progress: "You signaled that turn at a good spot." "Nice smooth stop this time." "Good recovery on that right turn." It was only by slowly gaining confidence in themselves as drivers that the most timid beginners were able to make informed but quick decisions pulling out of intersections, making left turns, or changing lanes. They gained confidence for the more complex maneuvers by building on the simple ones they could already do.

The social dimension of writing theory and practice is a given. But one aspect of that social dimension that is not taken seriously enough is respect for what learners already know and can already do. We may be so intent on problematizing social dimensions outside the classroom that we cannot see the social dimension of our own epistemological assumptions. In Freire's classes, which tapped into "multiple channels of communication," students saw themselves as already knowing something, as already capable of learning. Freire tapped into so many ways of knowing that everyone at some point must have felt validated and confident. This is no small thing. How much of our success in our career today is due to our confidence as learners? to the validation we received as makers of knowledge? Composition specialists today were most likely yesterday's linguistically talented students moving up in a linguisto-centric school system that privileged our way of knowing. But what if schools used only math or only drawing or only dance as a way of knowing? How would our word-loving brains have reacted? Would we have had the success in school and the confidence in ourselves we needed to seek higher degrees? to pour our energies into this language-loving discipline?

Many professors today proudly announce their own "rigor" and lament a "lowering of standards" on the part of their colleagues. In this atmosphere, it may be risky for professors, especially untenured ones, to broach the subject of student confidence in departmental discussions of teaching (in the unlikely event such discussions take place) because in our eager-to-essentialize culture, talking about confidence can quickly be constructed as "patronizing" students. Perhaps women need to use even more care than do men in articulating the importance confidence plays in learning because of the facile construction—and ultimate dismissal—of them as "nurturers." (See Eileen E. Schell's *Gypsy Academics and Mother-Teachers*.) Therefore, even professors who might see the importance confidence plays in knowledge making are constrained from promoting it publicly by deep-seated institutional prejudices against practice, against talk about practice, and perhaps even against promotion of student success.[8]

Paul Taylor is correct in his assertion that this concept, the importance of confidence in learning, is neither new nor original with Freire, who may have picked it up from John Dewey. But confidence may have had special meaning for Freire. Taylor cites O'Neill and Jarez and Hernadez Pico as suggesting that as a boy, Freire "was considered by some of his teachers to be mentally retarded" (14). If that is even partly true, Freire as a student must have known firsthand what it was like to have teachers hold insultingly low expectations. He may have known about the importance of confidence in ways not available to those used to having their linguistic talents privileged in traditional school methodologies. In *Talking Back*, bell hooks has also pointed to confidence as one of the "less obvious" obstacles students need to overcome if they are to invest the time and effort needed to write and revise their work. The opposite is also true: If students lack confidence and become completely discouraged, they will not engage.

The importance of confidence to learning, writing, and revising is also consistent with Robert Parker's and Vera Goodkin's argument that writers need some modicum of confidence that they will succeed if they are to embark on the process of reading, thinking, revising, and editing that good writing demands:

> To a considerable extent, far more than most teachers tend to believe, the quality of students' performance in various areas of the curriculum is directly tied to their views of themselves as learner/performers in that activity or discipline. (1987, 19)

Elza Freire's view of confidence, Parker and Goodkin's endorsement of it as necessary for student success, and bell hooks' view of confidence as a crucial element in the revising process, are all related to a point Freire makes in *Pedagogy of the Oppressed* regarding what he calls "self-depreciation":

> Self-depreciation is another characteristic of the oppressed, which derives from their internalization of the opinion the oppressors hold of them. So often do they hear that they are good for nothing, know

nothing, and are incapable of learning anything—that they are sick, lazy, and unproductive—that in the end they become convinced of their own unfitness. (49)

If students receive the spoken or unspoken message that their way of knowing is less than adequate, they may not have the heart to continue their education. Mina Shaughnessy knew that lack of confidence could fuel students' "fears that writing will not only expose but magnify [their] inadequacies." She also knew that writing "is, above all, an act of confidence, an assertion of the importance of what has gone on inside the writer . . ." (1977, 85). Amidst all the grandstanding that goes on today regarding "rigor" and "standards," it may be difficult to remember the role confidence plays in learning. Those who insist on thinking of everything in binary terms may say, "But we must have tough standards. We shouldn't patronize students by praising them for below standard work. We must keep expectations high." As this book will demonstrate, I have much to say about expectations, and keeping them high is one of the most important elements of teaching. And we can still have "tough standards," though that phrase by itself is meaningless without specific comparisons and examples of what those "tough standards" entail.

In an institution where I used to teach, one professor routinely pointed with pride to his place on the computerized grade rankings published by the institution each year. He gave the lowest grades in the college, so he was always at the bottom of the list, which he construed as prima facie evidence that he had the "highest standards." As far as I know, he did not discuss "standards" other than to announce that he had the highest ones. Never on the table for discussion were his specific expectations, assignments, exams, assessment criteria, or assumptions about what constituted knowledge or intellectual growth. I suspect that any mention of the role confidence plays in learning would have been dismissed as a capitulation to a "lowering of standards," without the fuss and bother of trying to define what they might be.

"Co-intentional" Learning

Teachers cannot simply *tell* students to be confident. Unless education is what Freire describes in *Pedagogy of the Oppressed* as "co-intentional," (56), with teachers learning from students and vice versa, students will rightly see empty praise as mere patronizing. The confidence students need must come from seeing themselves and their teachers as contributors and learners. Coming to know is an active, challenging process that requires self-awareness and metacognition. Anne E. Berthoff points out in her foreword to *Literacy: Reading the Word and the World:* "Peasants and teacher are engaged in dialogic action, an active exchange from which meanings emerge and *are seen to emerge:* it is central to Paulo Freire's pedagogy that learners are empowered by the knowledge that they are learners" (her emphasis, xiv). However, meanings cannot be "seen to emerge" without a live process: a dialogic atmosphere that cannot be faked. As Freire said, "It is not only a matter of teaching them, but also of learning from them" (1993, 123). Students and teachers must be "co-intentional" (1973, 56) learners, with problems posed to both groups: "The flow is in both directions" (1993, 125).

This co-intentional relationship is similar to the "horizontal relationship between persons," Freire discusses in *Education for Critical Consciousness* (45). Learning, dialectic, and challenge are all necessary for students *and* teachers, which is more likely to happen when teachers respect and use *all* language practices *and* all ways of knowing represented in the class, not simply the language practices and ways of knowing with which the English/writing teacher is most comfortable. Beth Daniell credits Berthoff for leading her to the following insight regarding what Daniell now sees as Freire's primary contribution to North American teachers: "an attitude of profound love for the human beings we teach. Being treated as if one is worth, as if one's life is important, as if what one has to say is significant and deserving attention" (1999, 402). In his essay in the *JAC* tribute issue, Henry Giroux wrote that Freire often quoted Che Guevara on the importance of love: "Let me tell you, at the risk of appearing ridiculous, the genuine revolutionary is animated by feelings of love. It is impossible to imagine an authentic revolutionary without this quality" (1997, 312).[9]

Twenty-five years ago, Mina Shaughnessy recognized the need for teachers to be learners. She said that teachers must "remediate" themselves and study the "students themselves in order to perceive both their difficulties and their incipient excellence" (238). In a class that encourages all ways of knowing available in that community of learners, all members of that community, including the teacher, would be challenged to work outside their comfort zone, and all would gain confidence in themselves as both learners and knowers. Unless teachers respect student knowledge and language practices, students will not have the confidence they need to take intellectual and political risks, to question the status quo, to reimagine a better world and work to achieve it. Unless teachers *believe* they can learn from their students, they'll end up *telling* students about oppression, and co-intentional education will become just another theoretical goal that is, in the end, separated from practice.

Commitment to, and Ongoing
Critique of, Taking Action

Perhaps because of Freire's faith in people and in the possibility of change, Freire was able to *both* critique social conditions as he saw them *and* to do something to change them. This taking of action, this committing to a pedagogy, is a courageous leap of faith. This commitment makes Freire's action, and his bold detailed articulation of it, vulnerable. It puts theorized practice on the table, under a bright light—where it is easy for others to examine it, dissect it, or knock it to the floor.

Freire knew, more than most educators even today, that what goes on *inside* a classroom is just as socially constructed and potentially oppressive as what goes on *beyond* a classroom. Unlike most academics past or present, Freire theorized the epistemological assumptions informing word-based pedagogies and found them potentially harmful. He therefore used a praxis that allowed for, and took advantage of, multiple ways of knowing, so that Freire himself would learn from his students, so that learning would be co-intentional and bi-directional, so that students would have confidence in what they already knew, so they would have the courage to challenge received cultural myths. He designed a practice consistent with his theory. But because clearly articulated, theorized pedagogies are so vulnerable to critique, it is rare to find them. Perhaps if it were not for Freire's "naive" faith in his students and in the possibility of change, we would not have the many writings and class descriptions that have done so much throughout the world to challenge banking-model methods, to promote critical literacy, and to inspire education reformers.

If Freire did speak occasionally of "truth" or "reality" in ways too unapologetically for the sensibilities of strict social constructivists of the twenty-first century, he would have no doubt welcomed any "contradictions" inherent in his worldview. Freire did not shrink from contradictory epistemologies. Contradictions regarding reality or truth or knowing were themselves consistent with his dialogically based praxis: that it is only through constant questioning and problematizing, even, perhaps especially, of our own theories/practices, that our work remains renewed and retheorized.

Further, if Freire's view of the world and of the constructedness of oppression was in conflict with his belief in a God or "truth" or "reality," he would have welcomed that contradiction as a way of keeping his praxis in flux, in dialogue with itself. In fact, in *Literacy: Reading the Word and the World*, Freire and Macedo talk of "social transformation" as "a historic process in which subjectivity and objectivity are united dialectically. There is no longer a way to make either objectivity or subjectivity absolute" (1987, 43).

This constant rethinking of one's praxis was a basic Freirean tenet: a process, a friction similar to what C. H. Knoblauch has described as "dialogue and commitment" (1988). Too much dialogue—without commitment to some kind of plan or approach—prevents any action *except* dialogue about practice/commitment. Too much fixed commitment/practice—without dialogue and constant self-reflection—prevents a commitment/practice from being ever changed or renewed. In addressing critiques that his practices did not "work" in the United States, Freire reminded the interviewer that his pedagogy is not portable, that a praxis can only grow out of educators remaking it each time and place in which they find themselves. He stressed that educators should be humble, should continue to learn, and should subject their own praxis to continuing inquiry. Being too certain—even of inevitable uncertainty—contradicts the spirit of Freire's praxis.

Freire's praxis demonstrates a stance toward culture that is at once critical and hopeful, assertive of its own view of the world but inviting of other views, committed to specific theories and practices, but subjecting them always to inquiry. In Composition today we need both skepticism and hope. We're too steeped in critique, too sure that it is others who are naive, too certain that other people's research is epistemologically flawed and therefore has nothing to add to our own. We're being too easy on ourselves.

Both/And Theories of Life and Knowing

It was perhaps Freire's varied intellectual interests that allowed him to not only tolerate but to work productively with contradictory epistemologies. As many have pointed out, different disciplines not only employ different discourses, but the discourses themselves are informed by different epistemological and evidentiary assumptions. As did other visionary reformers such as James Britton, Lev Vygotsky, and James Moffett, Paulo Freire had a broad interdisciplinary background. Taylor says Freire studied linguistics, law, philology, and communication theories (21). John L. Elias says that Freire was "an education philosopher, a philosopher of knowledge, a social critic, a sociologist of knowledge, an adult educator, a theologian of liberation, a theorist of revolution, . . . a phenomenologist, an existentialist, a Christian, and a Marxist" (31). This shows Freire comfortable with many views of the world and unafraid of contradictions or overlapping, even conflicting philosophies. He did not avoid binaries but welcomed them. He also called for interdisciplinarity. In *Pedagogy of the Oppressed,* when he is discussing how the theme of development might be used in the culture circles, Freire points out that this theme is not exclusive to one field:

The theme of development, for example, is especially appropriate to the field of economics, but not exclusively so. This theme would also be focalized by sociology, anthropology, and social psychology (fields concerned with cultural change and with the modification of attitudes and values—questions which are equally relevant to a philosophy of development). It would be focalized by political science (a field concerned with the decisions which involve development), by education, and so forth. (113)

Freire had a *both/and* epistemology (God and social construction); a *both/and* view of theory and practice (praxis); and a *both/and* view of commitment, coupled with ongoing inquiry regarding that commitment. These contradictory views, however, constantly in dialectic, are what kept his praxis fresh, always in renewal. These contradictory views of life, truth, knowledge, for which Freire has been criticized or dismissed as "naive," are ironically the very contradictions that forced his ongoing self-reflection and inquiry. These contradictions should be "embraced" (Elbow's term) for the dialectic we need to keep our own praxis less certain, to engage Freire's use of "multiple channels of communication," even if we do not understand them—in fact, *because* we do not understand them.

Notes

1. From *Literacy: Reading the Word and the World,* 1987, page 122.

2. See Elbow's *Embracing Contraries;* Berthoff's "Killer Dichotomies," in Ronald and Roskelly's *Farther Along,* as well as Zebroski's essay in the same volume, "Rewriting Composition as a Postmodern Discipline: Transforming the Research/Teaching Dichotomy."

3. See page 108 in Torres.

4. Quoted by Torres, her page 109. The reference appears to be from Freire's *The Politics of Education,* but no page number is given.

5. Quoted by Ira Shor p. 316 in "Education Is Politics: A Farewell to Paulo." *JAC* 17.3 (1997): 314–18. Shor cites p. 30 of *Learning to Question.*

6. Taylor raises the question regarding Freire's Culture Circles essentially to argue that they involved more indoctrination than most Freireans would like to believe. Others (Elias and Miller) have also suggested that the conclusions of the Culture Circle discussions were more foregone than accounts of Freire's work would have us believe. I do not address this critique here. I agree with Taylor, however, that Freire's classroom work has not been examined in depth.

7. In her contribution to *JAC's* tribute issue to Freire (17.3, 1997), Ann Berthoff argues that for the most part, Freire's insistence on theorizing teaching has not been understood. However, she says in a footnote that a group of people working in ESL and in Composition *do* understand Freire, and she

names those she says do: Elsa Auerbach, Nina Wallerstein, Patricia Laurence, Ann Raimes, Vivian Zamel, Beth Daniell, Louise Dunlap, Virginia Perdue, Kate Ronald, Hephzibah Roskelly, Dixie Goswami, Linda Shaw Finlay, and Valerie Faith. Berthoff also points out that all these people are women (309–10, "Remembering Paulo Freire").

8. Within the past year (2000), there was a WPA listserv discussion of a professor who thought a student must have plagiarized her paper because it was so well written. This was in spite of her having previously produced an entire portfolio of good writing, including drafts.

9. In "Remembering Paulo Freire" (*JAC* 17.3), Giroux cites Freire, p. 43 in *Pedagogy of Hope,* New York: Routledge, 1994.

Chapter Three

Strategies for Using Sketching, Speaking, Movement, and Metaphor to Generate and Organize Text

As we saw in Chapters 1 and 2, Composition could benefit from incorporating praxis that both recognizes and takes advantage of the different ways people come to know. Paulo Freire used his students' visual, tactile, and other literacies to help them develop language-based literacies. Some people do their best thinking without keyboards or pens. Even people who do think best using paper or screen can obtain intellectual insights by working outside familiar domains. This chapter suggests ways in which all writers who are in the early stages of a writing project can enhance their individual ways of knowing as they begin to generate, organize, and structure their ideas. It will suggest generating and organizing activities such as using "rhetorical proof cards," sketching-to-learn, oral peer response, metaphors, and oral journals that can both challenge and enhance conventional "writing process" strategies.

Many of us want our students to think more broadly, deeply, and critically as they generate a first draft or make the substantive changes an early draft often needs to become more sophisticated. The multisensory options in this chapter are designed to help *all* writers either generate ideas, or make "chain-saw" revisions (Elbow's phrase), the global reconceptualizations of a piece that can happen when people are able to obtain metacognitive distance—in other words, when writers can ponder the meaning of their meanings (to paraphrase Berthoff).

If learning to write, as Patricia Bizzell explains, "can be seen as a process of learning to think about one's own thinking" (1984, 453), it suggests that *other* ways to represent thinking about one's thinking could *also* be useful. Writing center work has already demonstrated the use of oral dialogue as a way for students to both articulate, analyze, and reshape their thinking. But drawing, graphing, and sculpting can also give people metacognitive distance on a project, as can physical movement. I propose that it is time for Composition as a field to re-think its dependence on writing as an inventing, shaping, and revising tool, and that we take more advantage of other ways of knowing students bring to our classes.

In order do this more challenging re-thinking, writers need to mentally step outside their ideas, to view them in another dimension. All writers need ways to challenge their first thoughts. As Freire wrote in *Education for Critical Consciousness*, "challenge is basic to the constitution of knowledge" (125). Challenge can spark insights for students as they think through what they might want to add, delete, move, change, or completely trash. To figure out what to do next at this initial, crucial stage, all writers can benefit from strategies that take them beyond conventional drafting routines.

For some of us, the act of *writing* a first draft is itself a way of organizing it. As we write, we are not merely recording our thoughts: We are discovering our ideas and getting insights regarding how to restructure or what to add to reinforce our claims. Peter Elbow has long argued that freewriting, reading the resulting text, finding its "center of gravity," and then beginning a new cycle of freewriting can work as an organizing and structuring tool. James Britton has shown how writing acts as a "shaping at the point of utterance," a way to discover ideas as well as to express them. Therefore, some writers do not need any other organizing heuristic than the first draft itself.

For other writers, a formal outline structure, available in most handbooks, can either help them get organized or motivate them to re-organize. Often, however, even for those who use writing itself as a heuristic, attempting a written outline is at best a ceremonial exercise done to satisfy the teacher after the paper has already been written. At worst it is an arbitrary straightjacket that locks the writer into a structure conceived before he or she has had a chance to think through more creative, productive options.

The following card-moving approach, which I call "rhetorical proof cards," can make organizing more useful to students with other-than-linguistic talents and more challenging to students who have become too comfortable with Roman-numeral-based outlines. It transforms what can be a lockstep, predictable structure into an unfamiliar, oral and kinesthetic group activity, which taps into different ways of knowing, suggests counterarguments, and gives further insights even to those who normally work well with conventional written outlines. It works equally well with first-year students, graduate students, and groups of high school teachers. It can work in conjunction with freewriting or with other organizing strategies such as brainstorming and clustering.

I first used it with first-year college students doing lengthy persuasive research papers, who were frustrated with the chaotic state of their collected notes: facts, statistics, expert opinions, as well as their own ideas. How could they arrange all this in a convincing argument? Drawing on the work of Ann Berthoff, who sees chaos as "generative," Cynthia Onore argues that the composing process, even learning itself, "is not possible without contraries, conflicts, and tensions" (1989, 240). At this point in their research project, these students had plenty of chaos. Forcing all their conflicting pieces of research into a conventional written outline too soon could make the complexities of the controversy appear to be more amenable to solution than they actually were. Written outlines, especially if attempted too soon, can truncate the fermenting action of not knowing how to organize an argument.

Keeping conflicts front and center for a while allows them to act as enzymes on thinking, stimulants to counter-intuitive thinking. Ideally, I wanted to find a way in which everybody could look at everyone else's notes, move them around physically, and play with all the various arguments that might be constructed. However, the logistics of photocopying even one student's full set of notes prevented me from trying this plan. Besides, the notes were handwritten, copious, and difficult to see all at once in a way that would facilitate discussion of concepts rather than details. There are computer programs in which students can write synchronistically on each others' papers, but for this discussion I didn't want people's faces locked on computer screens. To look at a whole paper would involve too much text. I wanted us to simultaneously obtain a global view of the text and play with individual sections of it, to relate part to whole. I wanted us to be able to physically manipulate large ideas as we were discussing them.

I no longer have students do the kind of research paper that initiated these rhetorical proof cards, but I use them in a variety of projects that require students to gain metacognitive distance on ideas.

Rhetorical Proof Cards

In order to help all of us play with the same ideas, I decided to produce notes with which we could all experiment.[1] I made up a set of hypothetical notes on the topic of capital punishment: general reasons for and against the death penalty, with the kinds of quotations, facts, case studies, and emotional news stories students would typically find if they were to research this topic in the library or on the Internet. (See Figure 3–1.)

The information in each box is put on a separate card, so that there are eighteen cards, each card with one of the above "notes."[2] I make enough of these eighteen-card packs so that each group of students will have its own set of cards. With these "notes" now on cards, students can easily manipulate them and discuss how they might arrange a paper given this hypothetical research.

Each group gets a pack of these eighteen cards, which they can spread out on a desk, table, or section of the floor so that they can all examine them together. I put students in groups of three or four—large enough for a good discussion but small enough so that each student has a good view of the cards and they can all reach the card outline they're putting together.

Here is the task: for the purpose of the exercise, the group must first decide whether the argument they construct with these notes will favor or oppose capital punishment. The one or two students who "go along" with the group's majority opinion for the sake of the exercise obtain a useful view of their opponent's main points. They also get insights on how they might order a counterargument. Once the group has decided on their hypothetical argument, they then arrange the cards in an outline order that makes sense. They may use the cards in any order, and they need not use every one. They are also told that there is no one right way to arrange the cards for either side of the argument, and of course, there is plenty of room for arguments along a continuum of extreme pro or con views of this issue.

After each group takes a few minutes to familiarize themselves with the cards, there begins much animated discussion about which ones to choose and where to place them. This exercise encourages students to consider radical organizational changes because it's very easy to move a card from the beginning of the outline to the end or the middle. They can also explore these questions:

- What happens when you use this hypothetical evidence as a straightforward series of reasons supporting capital punishment (the risk convicted murderers may kill prison guards; the desire some victims' families feel for retribution; popular appeals to justice, etc.)?

- How do the cards look as a linear list of reasons opposing capital punishment (the high cost of judicial appeals; the risk of executing innocent people; the lack of deterrent power, etc.)?

- How does either argument change when pro and con reasons are juxtaposed? (For example, the case of a released murderer killing

Figure 3–1
"Rhetorical Proof Cards" to move around as group constructs
arguments, counterarguments, and discusses ethics of rhetoric

Should capital punishment be abolished?	An account of a typical day in prison—a description of weight room, cafeteria, library, classroom.
Statistics showing how many people were murdered by released convicted killers.	Studies detailing the high cost of keeping someone in prison for life.
Statistics on the increase in murders in parts of the U. S. in recent years.	Grisly newspaper account of a child murdered by a convicted murderer out on parole after serving 10 years.
Graphic description of a murder committed by the most recently executed convicted murderer in U. S.	Quote from a woman whose son was murdered by a man who may be released in 2005.
Case study of a man who was electrocuted by the state of Alabama in 1957. In 1964, another man confessed to the same crime the executed man was convicted of committing.	Statistics suggesting capital punishment is not a deterrent.
A quotation from a priest/ minister/rabbi opposing capital punishment.	A quotation from a member of a murder victim's family saying that an execution will not bring the loved one back.
Studies showing that it costs more to execute a person than to keep him or her in prison for life.	Graphic description of death in a gas chamber.
A quotation from a member of a murder victim's family saying how relieved he is now that his loved one's murderer has been executed.	Facts showing that most countries have abolished capital punishment.
Statement by a Ph.D. philosopher opposing the death penalty.	Graphic description of an execution by electrocution.

again is immediately followed by facts showing capital punishment is not a deterrent.)

- How does the emphasis change if the order of those cards is reversed?
- What happens when you take an interesting case or shocking statistic and use it as an attention-getter in the opening paragraph?
- What happens when you use it to end the argument?

As rhetoricians are well aware, if readers can *feel* something, they may be more likely to change their minds. A successful argument can be built on logical reasoning as well as emotionally evocative examples. Structuring such an argument is best done with the collaborative insights of those good at abstract logic as well as those good at social empathy—those who know what is likely to capture readers' attention long enough to actually consider the argument and to move them emotionally in a way that will make them remember it. People with diverse voices and multiple insights will therefore greatly enrich a group discussion on effective rhetorical strategies.

The act of physically moving these cards around and a discussion of the effects of doing so makes the abstract job of organizing an effective argument into a visual, oral, and kinesthetic task to which students with a variety of talents can contribute. Students can be *told*, of course, about different ways to organize a paper. Moving these cards around, however, demonstrates to students the persuasive effects of adding, rearranging, or eliminating evidence. They can immediately see for themselves numerous rhetorical choices. Through sometimes heated group discussion, they discover how they might include a "fact" that works against their argument, and how they might counter it, or distract the reader by following it with a stronger or at least more startling piece of evidence.

In some groups, this exercise stimulates discussions of ethics. Should a fact or statistic supporting the opposite view be conveniently eliminated from an outline? After a discussion of possible rhetorical effects (i.e., Will informed readers think the writer is not aware of this counter argument and therefore is less credible?), the group can explore possible ethical issues involved in deliberately excluding crucial evidence. Is the ultimate goal of the argument to persuade readers to agree with the writer or to fully explore the controversy in a way that will enlighten both supporters and opponents? Do the ends of persuasion justify the means? These are complex questions that force students to grapple with infinite choices, making them think critically about the implications of placing, moving, eliminating, or including even one card.

After the groups have negotiated the order of the cards, we take turns having a spokesperson from each group explain their outline, their reasons for the placement they chose, and the most interesting problems or conflicts the group had to solve as they organized the cards. This large group discussion impresses on the entire class the many possible ways an argument could be constructed, even when groups might be arguing the same view.

The real value in this exercise comes in the small-group disagreements on what evidence they should include, change, move, foreground, bury, end with, or eliminate. Because it is an oral discussion, students who speak more eloquently than they write have a chance to contribute valuable insights. The confidence they gain from contributing to this sophisticated oral analysis of organizational, rhetorical strategies will affect how they approach their next individually written draft. If they can order ideas in a discussion, the idea of ordering them on paper seems less daunting.

Students already comfortable with formal written outlines may gain the most from this exercise. Conventionally good writers, some of whom may speak with less confidence than that with which they write, are challenged to articulate their ideas verbally. This is good for them. Even good writers, accustomed perhaps to succeeding in school without having to verbalize much, must learn to speak up and participate in a lively debate. More important, these small groups tap into everyone's brain power. In debating organizational strategies, students gain valuable perspectives they would have missed if everyone were silently working on individual formal written outlines, concentrating on whether to use a Roman numeral or capital letter. This exercise transforms the abstract task of "organization" into a visual, verbal, and physical give-and-take as students move ideas around like pieces in a puzzle. It is an intellectual task as well as a physical one, as students much reach across the table to add, rearrange, or move groups of cards.

This exercise challenges students to tap into a variety of thinking patterns. Linguistically talented writers accustomed to a safe but formulaic way of writing will gain insights on alternate ways of organizing and be encouraged to risk a more interesting structure. Those who excel at composing well-constructed sentences and paragraphs might benefit from a mathematically oriented person who can analyze complex concepts and manipulate logical patterns. Kinesthetic learners who move the cards around on the floor or desk can begin to think of written texts as less monolithic and more like a series of related, changeable sections that are physically malleable. Those who speak well but might not be meticulous editors and proofreaders—and therefore might think of themselves as "bad" writers—can excel in these discussions in a way that gives them confidence and motivation when they return to their own notes. Socially talented learners who are good at reading people can help the group consider possible emotional effects on readers of beginning or ending an essay with the use of a particular fact, statistic, or case study. Everyone is included. Everyone is challenged.

After animated small-group and large-group discussion in which the instructor can direct these new insights back towards individual projects, students can return to their own research with a more sophisticated sense of organizational possibilities. As they bring their essays from early to developed drafts, they may be more likely to make structural revisions or complete start-overs. With the insights gained from this card exercise, students will now be more aware of how they can best take advantage of cut-and-paste word processing or hypertext technology to reconceptualize their own work.

This exercise not only allows those with a variety of talents to work in a domain that might be more amenable to their thinking patterns than is a text-based lesson on outlining. More importantly, it challenges those used to writing or organizing in predictably safe patterns to awaken some different brain cells and stretch their intellects by viewing textual possibilities through alternate perspectives. It teaches sophisticated concepts through a literally hands-on approach that challenges "at-risk" learners and academically talented students alike.

Sketching-to-Learn

The sketch was another way of looking at where I was in comparison with where I wanted to be in this paper.

—Melanie (in her metacognitive
analysis of a writing project)

Another alternative to traditional ways of organizing a draft is to have writers sketch, draw, or graph the shape of their ideas, using no words or as few words as possible. In their presentation at the 1999 Writing Across the Curriculum Conference at Cornell University, as mentioned earlier, Pam Childers and Eric Hobson added a "ninth intelligence"—the visual—to Howard Gardner's eight. They said using students' ability to draw could be used more in writing classes. In their book, *ARTiculating: Teaching Writing in a Visual World,* Childers, Hobson, and Joan Mullin describe a number of concrete activities designed to incorporate visual learning with writing, to stimulate both invention and revision. In her essay, "Alternative Pedagogy: Visualizing Theories of Composition," Joan A. Mullin shows how a class visit to an art museum and a discussion about its structure and function afterwards using "the language of architecture" can help students think metaphorically about the architecture and structure of their essays. The visit and subsequent discussion regarding function and structure is a three-dimensional, visual and kinesthetic experience that can help writers think in a different perspective about the purpose and organization of their writing.

In the same text, Eric H. Hobson describes a teachers' workshop in which the participants must construct "a storyboard of at least six one-frame cartoons," representing how they arrived at the workshop. By then rearranging the frames, eliminating some, and adding more details in others, the participants use visual and kinesthetic inroads to both generate and reorganize their narratives. They may also be asked to "zoom" in on one section of one of the frames, where a detail is particularly important. They then re-sketch or add to that one area (144–46). All writers, whether or not they are visual learners, can then transfer to their writing or revising the concepts of reorganization, example, detail, transition, elaboration, etc.

I have been using sketching in my writing classes for a number of years now because of positive reactions to the following activity, for which I am indebted to Kathy Iannone, a student I had at Utica College of Syracuse University in an independent study course designed to prepare undergraduate English majors for student teaching. In the unit on organization she was teaching in my first-year writing class, she took advantage of her background in art to design the following non-linguistic exercise. I use a version of it regularly now in all my classes.

This activity works best when students already have initial concepts or even completed research, but may be frustrated in trying to organize their ideas or locate their main purpose. Sketching, drawing, or graphing developing ideas gives students who can visualize images an opportunity to use that talent productively. It forces those comfortable with words to see their text through a different perspective. For both experienced and novice writers, this unconventional mode can work with or against their customary thinking patterns, producing valuable insights regarding overall purpose, structure, use of evidence, etc.

Student Sketches

The first sample sketches are from two advanced exposition classes in which students are working on an involved seven-week, ten- to twelve-page project. In the written assignment that the sketches below represent, students are asked to locate a controversy in their area of interest, read letters to the editor representing the various sides, and then analyze the letters from a rhetorical perspective. To learn how to analyze texts in this way, we read a number of similar analyses, do some "live" analyzing in class, and discuss why such analysis is worthwhile.

I ask students to do this assignment for several reasons. By studying how rhetorical strategies work, students are less likely to be vulnerable to the power of discourse. They learn to read these letters and other texts with an alertness to how and why writers choose words, studies, experts' opinions, and other rhetorical proofs, as well as to how ethos is constructed. Being conscious of rhetorical strategies in others' writing theoretically makes students more conscious of them in their own. By studying all the sides in the controversy the letters represent, students learn that issues are more complex than they originally thought, and that "facts" can be picked and chosen and arguments constructed and reconstructed. Finally, I take them through these seven weeks of writing, responding, and revising, so that they will leave this class convinced that peer response is worthwhile and revising is necessary. The primary task in this project is to analyze the rhetorical strategies used in the different arguments. Students do not need to take a side themselves; their purpose is to convince readers that their rhetorical analysis is valid.

Students produced the sketches discussed below after they had received substantial responses to their drafts, from me and from other students, but before the final drafts were due. They were asked to sketch, graph, or draw the organization of their papers so far, and/or an alternate organization. They could also visually represent a problem they saw in their papers or noticed in the letters they were analyzing. They had about fifteen minutes of class time to do this.

In response to this prompt, Terri focused on problems she saw in her draft: that her analysis might be too repetitious and her ending too boring. She sketched a doctor with crash-cart paddles trying to revive a dying patient. She explained, "Reader interest then drops way down because can't think of how to conclude. Needs shock (jolt) like doctor gives patient when crashing." (See Figure 3–2.)

Another student used the exercise to represent something she noticed about the letters to the editor she was analyzing. Ali drew a Venn diagram[3] illustrating what she calls "Patterns in Letters." (See Figure 3–3.)

Ali's Venn diagram illustrates how the "pro" letters overlap with the "con": "In every letter for the argument there is some part that states a con. For every con letter there is some part that states a pro issue." I do not know if being asked to represent the letter patterns triggered her seeing them, or if she saw them before and this was simply a way to represent what she had already discovered. However, doing this diagram and/or explaining it in class might have helped her articulate it more clearly in her paper. What's more, her sketch and explanation might trigger in other students insights into the letters they are analyzing.

Figure 3–2
Conclusion needs "crash cart"

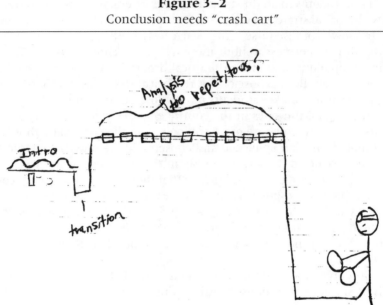

Figure 3–3
Ali's Venn diagram showing pro and con overlap in
letters to the editor

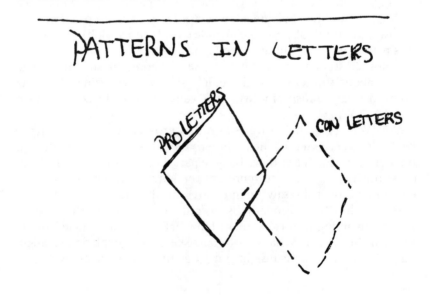

Another student, Jay, sketched his draft's "Current Structure" on the left side of his page and an alternate "Possible Structure" on the right side. (See Figure 3–4.) Jay did not have time to explain the new framework, but he described the original: "In the current structure each article refers back to others before it in a sequential order. This

Figure 3–4

The current structure of Jay's draft and a possible revised structure

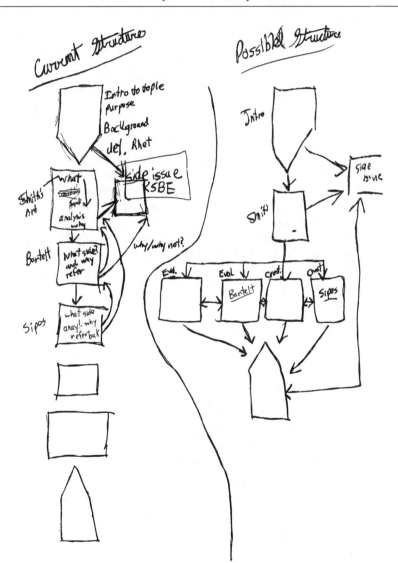

structure is based on chronology of publication of the letters. It gives a 'real time' sense of analysis." As we can see in his "Possible Structure," however, the four boxes in a horizontal line show that the analyses of the letters will no longer appear in simple time order, like floats in a parade. Instead, he will intermix them and relate them to a conclusion, represented by a box with a point targeted back to the now-blended analysis. They will also be related to a "side issue" near the beginning.

Jay put a version of these sketches up on the white board, explaining that he was going to change the whole structure. Slightly horrified, one student said, "But won't you have to cut and paste huge chunks and move things around?" Jay answered yes, but didn't seem perturbed by this. I added, "That's the whole point. You do need to consider some rearrangement of your different analyses in your paper."

Ultimately, Jay did not use the new structure represented here but continued to play with different possibilities. What is valuable about these sketches, though, is that they provide a thumbnail way to conceptualize and discuss important aspects of a work-in-progress without having to read through six to ten pages of text to discern an overview. They also inspire others to make big structural changes by providing a kind of satellite picture of draft geography, enabling students and responders to discuss global issues rather than the spelling of a street sign.

Several students used the sketches to discover or represent global problems they encountered in their projects. Natalie's rhetorical analysis involved the controversial Enola Gay exhibit at the National Air and Space Museum (NASM). In her sketch, our eyes are drawn to a stick figure in the lower left, the writer, who has a sad face and a bubble caption, "Information overload." (See Figure 3–5.)

In her words:

> My sketch is the "Enola Gay" (the airplane that dropped the atomic bomb on Hiroshima), dropping the "Journal of American History" issues from Dec. 1995 and March 1996. The "Enola Gay" is dropping the *AH [Journal of American History]* bomb symbolically on the National Air and Space Museum (NASM). There is fire in the windows of the museum, showing that the "Enola Gay" exhibit was "bombed" or crushed (cancelled). The "Enola Gay" is also dropping the "AH" on me. I am struggling & frustrated because the "bomb" has so much information my brain is on information overload and I have a tremendous amount of information to plow through.

I cannot say if doing this sketch helped Natalie with her subsequent drafts, but the depiction of the writer's dismay regarding having too much information may have helped her focus on a problem to solve in her draft. In a metaphor she wrote describing the process, she again brings up the idea of excess:

Figure 3–5
Natalie's "information bomb" overloading her brain

Writing a rhetorical analysis is like weeding a garden. All things can grow in a garden, but only the important vegetables can stay because they bring life to the garden. They are what a person will eat. A person will not eat weeds, they do not taste good. They tend to kill the vegetables in the garden. A garden can get overgrown with weeds so much that the vegetables can not be seen anymore.

Figure 3–6
Matt's graph of predicted readers' interest

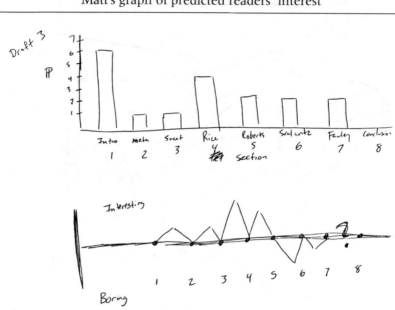

Natalie uses the "weeding" or "plowing through" metaphor again in the metacognitive analysis she did when the paper was completed. First she notes, "This project was, by far, the most complex piece of writing that I have done at the university." In addition to "weeding out" the overload of information she referred to in her sketch and in her metaphor, she also had to sort through comments from her classmates: "The peer responses helped me and I weeded out some of the advice because of the fact that not everyone will agree with everything that has to change in the paper."

Matt Vaughn came right out and said that sketching his draft helped him make decisions about revising. (See Figure 3–6.)

Here is Matt's explanation of the graphs:

Sketch 1 at the top of the page represents the number of paragraphs allotted in the text for each section. By this sketch, I could see that the introduction and the Rice letter were both heavy, and that the meta-analysis and coverage of the Sweet letter were light. I have since attempted to fix this problem in the final draft.

Sketch 2 at the bottom of the page rates the relative interest I thought a reader would have in the various sections of the draft. Interesting sections have peaks at the top, and boring sections make valleys in a

Figure 3–7
Katie trying to balance casual and academic discourse

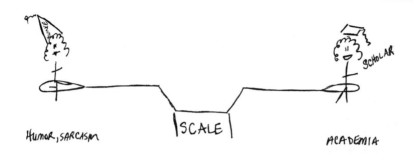

modified line graph. I found the Fawley and Szalavitz sections a little boring and tried to fix them. Additionally, I added a conclusion, noted as absent by the question mark.

In his metacognitive analysis, Matt explains that the "largest change" he made in his subsequent draft was to delete almost completely the section on Szalavitz, which his graph helped him realize was "boring." He also reread her letter, found "more interesting (and more subtle) strategies," and analyzed those instead. He says that section of his paper is "much stronger now." He explains how the sketch helped him:

> I did learn an interesting tidbit from sketching out the draft how I thought it would be visually represented. Though my graph form is highly unoriginal, it pointed out to me more clearly what parts were too thick and too thin. In a related graph, I could easily see what parts I personally found boring and those that kept my attention. If I could bore myself in places, I was fairly certain I'd lose the reader.

Katie's sketch addresses the problem of balancing everyday language and academic language. Interestingly, in Matt's metacognitive analysis, he named Katie's essay as the one whose "tone and language" caught his attention immediately. (See Figure 3–7.)

Katie's sketch shows a scale balancing "casual discourse," such as humor and sarcasm, and academic discourse. The humor/sarcasm side shows a female stick figure wearing a dunce cap. The academic side shows a female "scholar" wearing a mortarboard.

Sketching helped these students isolate global problems before they became bogged down in editing. It helped provide a quick but distanced analysis of major issues to be solved during the final weeks of the project.

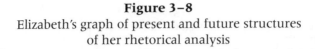

Figure 3–8
Elizabeth's graph of present and future structures
of her rhetorical analysis

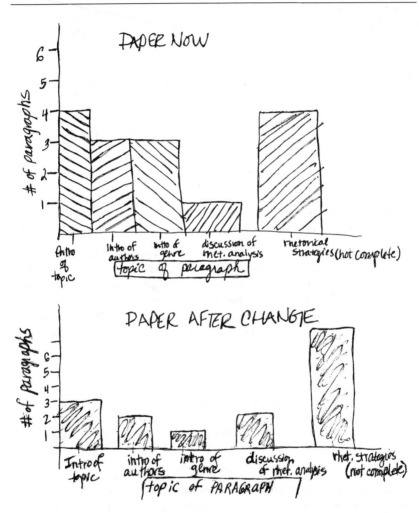

I also experimented with sketching in an upper level, rhetorical theory class. Here students were also doing rhetorical analysis, but they were analyzing much longer and more complex essays than were my advanced exposition students. In the above illustration, Elizabeth graphs her paper's present organization as well as its projected organization after major changes she is making. When she did this, she was about midpoint in that (ten- to twelve-page) rhetorical analysis project. (See Figure 3–8.)

Here is her explanation:

At this point in the project, I was having a lot of trouble with the introduction of the topic, the authors, and the terminology. I already had five pages, and I had not even started the actual analysis itself.

I knew that there was a lot I needed to cut from the introduction, and even more I needed to do with the rhetorical analysis.

I decided to make a bar graph. Both graphs had "Number of Paragraphs" on the vertical axis and "Topic of Paragraph" on the horizontal axis. The first graph was titled "Paper Now," and the second, "Paper After Change." The bars within the graph represent how many paragraphs were written for each part of the draft.

In the first graph, the tallest bars are over the introduction sections. In the second graph, the tallest bar is over the rhetorical analysis section of the draft.

By counting the paragraphs devoted to different sections of her current draft and then graphing them, Elizabeth was able to get a visualization of how "top-heavy" her introduction was as well as how she needed to streamline her opening pages so that she could foreground *analysis* in what she knew should take up the bulk of the paper. I cannot say, of course, that having Elizabeth do this exercise gave her an insight about revision that a class discussion or teacher commentary might not have given her. I can say that it took only about ten minutes of class time, and that her model might be used in the future to help students rethink their own focus in their drafts.

Sometimes graphing one's progress in organizing can lead to insights regarding the direction of the paper. Having students put their sketches on a white board or on an overhead and then have them explain them to the class can help everyone rethink the organization or frame of their own work. When students talk through their sketch, they often pinpoint a problem, even if they don't instantly solve it. Also, after doing a visual representation of their ideas, some students invent original metaphors to use in a subsequent draft, as we will see. Thinking and working with ideas in words and images, and then explaining them orally, increases opportunities for insight. Sketching, graphing, or drawing a concept, or representing part of it as a metaphor, can challenge everyone in a class. Just the attempt is worthwhile. For some visual learners or language-learning disabled students, generating and/or representing ideas imagistically may allow them to work in a format more appropriate to their intellectual process, their way of knowing. It may do for them what freewriting does for people who prefer to play with ideas in words and sentences. For those people who do think in words—being asked to sketch a draft may prod brain cells not used to carrying their weight. The resulting neuron stretch may contribute insights writers may not have discovered through a conventional written outline—a tool which for them may have become too easy.

Metaphors

Sketches tap into different areas of the brain, as do metaphors. Sometimes when students do sketches, it generates metaphors they use in revisions. For example, in the same advanced exposition class mentioned earlier, students in the first few weeks of the semester were doing a short (three- to four-page) essay on academic discourse. They had a number of options: responding to readings by Gerald Graff, Mike Rose, Robin Tolmach Lakoff, and June Jordan from the *Living Languages* collection of essays; writing about their own adventures with academic discourse, with brief references to the texts we read in class; analyzing writings from different textbooks they were using in other courses; some combination of those, or an idea of their choosing, provided it had something to do with academic discourse and the power-related issues we were discussing in class.

About halfway through the project, I asked the students to draw, sketch, freewrite, or make a simile or metaphor describing academic discourse. To write the metaphor, they were to finish a sentence that begins, "Academic discourse is like . . ." and then explain the sentence. Everyone did a sketch. No one freewrote. Some came up with a metaphor after they had done a sketch. The point was to approach their work so far from a different angle, to conceive it holistically, but sideways or upside down, or through a different medium.

Students' Sketches Generating Metaphors

Melissa did an interesting sketch as a way to rethink her first draft: a letter aimed at incoming first-year students, discussing the language(s) used in college. Such a letter might be included in a packet of materials given out at orientation. In her sketch, there is a student driving a car that just had a recent gasoline fill-up. (See Figure 3–9.)

The fuel is represented by alphabet letters; the metaphor is that academic language powers a student's success in college. She had a student driving a car, with the fuel being the language used in college. Above the sketch she explains it:

> It seems as if we are striving to reach a common goal, and we are powered by the academic language in our discourse to be the fuel that drives us to the top.
>
> Language and the development of our language in academia hurdles us over the top barrier that might stand in the way of achieving membership status in our career or work field.

Underneath the sketch, she raises a question for herself and makes revising plans:

> Why is this so important? Now I want to add a paragraph on why academic language is so important to students and how it will help them

Figure 3–9
Melissa's sketch that generated a metaphor

achieve status in their future career goals. Somewhere after the professor paragraph.

She later added that metaphor to her final draft, near the end of her letter to incoming students:

> Language is the power that will take you to the next level in your academic life. It will allow you to become a member of the distinguished group of English majors or an elite group of biochemical engineers. It seems as if each student is striving to reach a common goal, and the academic language powers us in our discourse to achieve that goal. The language becomes the fuel that drives us to the top. Language and its development in academia hurdles us over the top barrier that might stand in the way of achieving status in our future career.

It is not my purpose here to do an in-depth "before and after" analysis of Melissa's early drafts and the one she ultimately handed in for a grade. I can say, however, that the car-with-language-as-fuel metaphor did not appear in either of her early drafts of this project, written five days earlier than the final version, and before we did the sketching activity in class. Her third and final version is longer than the

earlier drafts and has a completely revamped opening and closing section—with many paragraphs inserted and others changed.

In the new version, Melissa also added a new paragraph to her introduction, structuring it around another new analogy: "Language and
communication is what defines a culture. If we think of a major as a
culture, we can say that the language used in that discourse identifies
that major from another major." Later in that paragraph, she continues
the analogy, weaving it into the last sentence of the paragraph: "As in
any culture, it is the common language that ties people together, just as
it can place a barrier between an outsider that does not understand the
language being spoken." Interestingly, the language-as-culture analogy
was not part of the language-as-fuel sketch and metaphor she did in
class. It may be, however, that doing the sketch and visualizing the car
metaphor stimulated her thinking in ways that helped her to think
analogously, to "see" other connections.

In fact, in the metacognitive statement she handed in with her final
draft, Melissa credits class activities with helping her reconceive her
work: "After taking into consideration all of the activities we did in
class, I took the new ideas I came up with and applied them to my paper." She uses yet another metaphor in her explanation: "After doing
the activities in class, I saw this paper in a much different light. It was
almost as if each activity was a door, and behind that door stood more
insight on how to further develop my paper."

In the same class, for the same assignment (on academic discourse),
another student used her in-class sketch, and the metaphor it triggered,
to revise her essay. Terri sketched a simple cartoon, stick figures of a giant professor and a tiny student. The caption reads "Academic Language and Power (from the student's point of view)." The sketch shows
the student getting relatively larger as she or he learns academic discourse (see Figure 3–10).

In her note to herself after doing the sketch, Terri wrote:

Ideas to Use in Paper
Explain the changes in feelings of students as they start achieving or
even mastering the academic discourse that originally alienated them.
Make this more visual in minds instead of implying it. Tell how learning academic discourse empowers students.

In her final draft, which was a letter to a neighbor back home who
was going to college next year, she added this simile, which did not appear in her earlier draft: "Until you start to learn the discourse, you can
feel very small and powerless in class, like a tiny bug listening to a powerful giant (the professor) speak." She returns to the image in one of
her final paragraphs: "As you put extra effort into learning the dis-

Figure 3-10
Terri's sketch that generated a metaphor

course that surrounds you in college, you will begin to feel empowered. After a time you may even laugh at yourself as your remember that tiny bug feeling you once had while in the face of the 'giant' professors." Terri clearly is able to use the stick-people cartoon she sketched in a few minutes and turn it into a metaphor that helps fulfill her instruction to herself to make what academic discourse does to people "more visual in minds instead of implying it."

The metaphors these sketches can generate help students gain metacognitive distance on their projects. Metaphors can help students recast an argument, and/or they can be added to a revision to enhance an explanation, as we have seen in Melissa's and Terri's essays.

The Power of Metaphor Underused

George Lakoff's and Mark Johnson's work on the importance of metaphor is well known. In their 1980 text, *Metaphors We Live By,* they say that metaphors involve thought and action as well as language: "Our ordinary conceptual system, in terms of which we both think and act, is fundamentally metaphorical in nature" (3). Others have pointed out the importance of metaphor. Eleanor Kutz and Hephzibah Roskelly point out that metaphor "is so ubiquitous in the language and in thinking that most people don't recognize it as a strategy that allows them to name and control reality" (230). Michael Bruner and Max Oelschlaeger credit Richard Rorty in *Objectivity, Relativism, and Truth* for arguing that metaphor is vital to moral and intellectual growth (216).

Sharon Crowley and Deborah Hawhee point out that most grammar handbooks are not as a rule concerned with "extraordinary uses of language" such as metaphors or other figures of speech (229). However, they cite Quintilian's view that figures of speech can make language more clear than it might be without them (229). They remind us that figurative speech serves a powerful rhetorical function and that conventional textbook writing pedagogies do not foreground it enough (232, 263). S. Michael Halloran and Annette Norris Bradford also critique conventional pedagogies in rhetoric and technical writing that discourage the use of metaphor. They argue that "a judicious use of figures—both schemes and tropes—is warranted in scientific and technical writing" (180). The gap these scholars point to might be partially addressed by having students sketch in the way described.

I frequently use metaphor to help students gain insights regarding rhetorical analysis. As mentioned earlier, students in my advanced exposition class were analyzing the rhetoric used in letter-to-the-editor exchanges regarding a controversy of their choosing (i.e., the moratorium on the Illinois death penalty as discussed in *The Chicago Tribune* letters to the editor; the Amadou Diallo shooting in New York City and the op/ed pages of *The New York Times;* the "grammar" debate in opinion pieces and letters in *English Journal*).

As students entered the final phase of these projects, however, there were still many who were not taking enough advantage of interesting rhetorical strategies they found and/or were belaboring the obvious. For example, they were simply repeating what a sentence said rather than how it worked rhetorically, or they were simply supporting or arguing with a claim the author made, or with the reasons, rather than examining how the claim and support for it work in the particular rhetorical context. For this project, they were to look more closely at things such as word choice, syntax, placement, connotation, etc., and discuss a writer's rhetorical choices. Sometimes a section of their drafts would do that, but there was a lot of uncompelling summarizing and paraphrasing instead of insightful analysis. At this point, they needed a strategy for helping them decide what to elaborate on and what to delete.

During previous class discussions, I had discussed a microscope analogy:

> In this rhetorical analysis, think of the reader as someone looking through your microscope. You, the writer/and rhetorical analyst, are standing next to him or her, explaining what the reader sees under your slide. You point things out. You explain how they work. With that metaphor in mind, read through your draft and ask yourself this: If there are things the reader could see without the help of your lens and your explanation, don't spend much time and space explaining them. But if the reader would not be aware of these strategies except for your putting them under the lens and explaining them, then by all means elaborate on those strategies. Take some time to point them out and show how they work. Don't belabor the obvious. Do belabor the not-obvious.

I thought of another metaphor: "Writing a rhetorical analysis is like analyzing a basketball game." Someone who had never been to a basketball game would notice players running up and down the court and occasionally throwing the ball in the net. A coach or experienced player would see complex plays and moves leading up to the shot. Sitting next to the novice, the coach or experienced player could explain things, helping the novice "see" strategies in the game that had been invisible before, except to a trained eye. To extend the metaphor: If there are moves in the game (text) that any observer would notice, don't spend time on it. If there are moves in the game (text) that the average reader needs explicated, that's where you want to elaborate.

Then we took a few minutes for students to come up with their own analogy. I said to begin with this phrase: "Writing a rhetorical analysis is like _____ ing . . ," and to insert a verb in the blank. Then explain the analogy and how it might work to sort and select sections of their drafts to delete or elaborate on. After I gave them a few minutes to come up with these similes, people read or talked about them orally. Here is what some people wrote (or said):

> Writing a rhetorical analysis is like
>
> . . . a florist selecting roses for bouquets and arrangements. Someone who doesn't know what they should be looking for might miss certain

details. For instance, are their seeples tipped up or down? Are they tight or blown? Are they holding color or are they brown in spots? Are the stems cut at an angle? All of these questions address how long the roses will last in a fresh bouquet or arrangement. —Diana

. . . sorting through Halloween candy in your pumpkin. You must sort it thoroughly, separate it into groups . . . some pieces don't belong . . . some are similar, some you've never seen before and have to examine closely (look at the words, the ingredients, etc.), and look it over twice before you decide whether you want it or not. Once you've got it all sorted and organized, you're ready to peel apart the wrapper and the stuff you're going to throw away. —Deb

. . . scuba diving in the ocean; you have to have an experienced diving instructor in order to get the most out of your trip. —Michelle

. . . watching a Spike Lee movie. —Anita

. . . writing your own wedding vows. —Dorene

. . . investigating the motive in a murder mystery. —Cathy

. . . looking for change in a couch. —Matt

It was fun listening to the creative analogies people came up with. More important, it gave writers struggling with a difficult assignment a way to think about it in a different, yet also familiar, way. Although metaphors involve written language, when students elaborate on them, we could all imagine the sounds, smells, or physical activity the metaphor described. Metaphors stimulate alternate ways of thinking because as Lakoff and Johnson point out, "The essense of metaphor is understanding and experiencing one kind of thing in terms of another" (5).

Using metaphors, and the multiple channels they approximate, promotes a classroom synergy that is more than the sum of its parts. Everyone benefits from the active brainwork of everyone else. With its frequent and unusual perspective shifts, this metaphoric thinking challenges many intelligences.

Oral Outlining or Previewing

In the same way a graphic or metaphoric representation of an idea might help students think in different ways about a writing project, an oral preview or outline can trigger useful insights. Asking students to verbalize their plans for, or problems with, an upcoming writing project can also work like jumper cables to the imagination, especially as students hear others work through their writing problems orally. In-class oral previewing or problem solving can take from twenty minutes to an hour of class time, but is well worth the investment. If time allows, and the class is not too large, students might sit in a large circle and take one or two minutes each to address questions raised by the teacher. It gets everyone to contribute in relative safety—no one need stand in front of the class, "oral report" fashion. They may stay in their desks, and they need not prepare anything more than an early draft or informal outline.

As students talk and listen, they begin to generate ideas and to identify problems and strengths in their work so far. As they and others weave in references to class readings or discussions, students begin to see connections between old and new knowledge. Talking about their project can convince them they *do* have something important to say, and it can help them begin to say it. In addition, as teachers hear these early ideas, they can quickly determine which students are well on their way to a substantive first draft, and which students are yet not focused enough. Getting students to talk about their projects, therefore, helps writers see where they want to go and simultaneously helps teachers see which students need the most help in getting there. When students hear that their classmates have important stories to tell, or arguments to make, they are also more likely to trust them later when they respond to written drafts. As Marie Ponsot and Rosemary Deen point out, when students listen to each other read from or talk about their individual handling of a class project, they "have a personal basis for being more concerned listeners, colleagues really, engaged with similar experiences in similar enterprises with no loss of individual difference" (1982, 17). If class time is at a premium, the teacher could divide students into small groups or pairs. Students would address the same questions orally, but it might take only three to ten minutes of class time. The teacher could circulate, hearing as many dialogues as possible.

Oral previewing or problem raising can help spark ideas. If, for example, one student hears another talking about a particularly memorable visit with a grandparent, he or she might remember a parallel incident with a favorite aunt or younger cousin. If one student hears another relate the excitement of a tournament basketball game, he or she might remember getting that last important spare in a highest-score bowling game. Hearing someone else talk about particular sights or sounds from a vivid incident might remind students to add such sensory details to their own narratives, or examples to their arguments. Such expansions are the "collocations" that Witte and Faigley have shown are present in high-rated essays in the research they summarized (1981, 193).

This kind of verbalizing is relevant to something Lester Faigley argues in *Fragments of Rationality*. His view, which I partly accept, is that

Composition has not embraced postmodern notions of multiple selves. He sees Composition foregrounding the modern (as opposed to post-modern) notion of an individual "self," and perhaps he would say that this exercise plays to such notions of individuality. While it's true that this verbalizing foregrounds individual reports, it also recognizes that these are people whose subject positions create different degrees of confidence, fear, and familiarity with academic conventions of analysis and argument. The voicing of these fears seems to calm those most worried about "not doing it right," at the same time the variety of proj-ects discussed demonstrates that there is no one "right" way. The vo-cabulary of analysis used in these talks reassures writers that others are in the same relative boat: riding the ups and downs of this project, searching for a compass. It also provides a guiding buoy to those drift-ing into shallow inlets of summary, when they should be exploring the open ocean of analysis.

Oral outlining or previewing can also take place outside of class. Students might meet in groups with questions to address, or take part in organized telephone interviews with their peers regarding their projects. Having the teacher present in a class discussion helps fore-ground threads that will help the largest number of people, but the point is to take more advantage of verbalizing, with or without the teacher.

Most important, oral previewing or problem-solving privileges *stu-dent* voice, an element Robert Parker has argued is essential to students' intellectual development. In his critique of how the London-based lan-guage program got turned into writing across the curriculum programs in this country, Parker wrote, "Here people have been quite exclusively concerned with writing: other uses of language have been totally ne-glected" (1985, 174). What's more, Parker says, by not taking more advantage of the role Vygotsky says speech plays in language develop-ment, schools are limiting students' intellectual growth: "When op-portunities for dialogue are limited by the structure and content of classroom language, then, it would seem, the growth of the mind is curtailed" (1982, 12).

Oral Journals

Because I've seen the value of talk in writing and revising, I now also use some form of oral journals or reading logs in all my classes. I usu-ally have students respond to readings, class discussions, or assignment progress by having them do a variety of in-class and out-of-class activ-ities. For example, in addition to having them keep some kind of written reading log or journal, or e-mailed response, I also have them keep an oral journal or do an oral response.[4] Office voice mail is the most practical option because students can call at any time, without disturbing anyone, and the instructor can access it at any time. On a rotating basis, groups of students call my voice mail and respond to a problem I've given them. I might ask questions about a difficult reading, for example, or for an update on a writing project. To prevent the tape from filling up, the students can be asked to call at different times, or the teacher can listen to the messages at regular intervals, taking notes and deleting the messages regularly. Students do not hear each other with the voice-mail option, but the teacher can take notes on the gist of the messages and relate selected comments the next day.

With voice mail, instructors can listen closely to each student, playing the message again if necessary, or saving it to respond to later. Hearing students' voices through a receiver, instead of from across a classroom, allows the teacher to hear nuances of meaning in word selection, pauses, and tone. It gives teachers a better sense of who is confidently moving ahead on the project, and who is frustrated, confused, or completely stalled. And students can speak uninterrupted on tape, editing it or starting over if they want to. In addition, voice mail automatically limits long-winded speakers (though I tell them they can call back and continue their message if they are initially cut off), while students who are very nervous formulating thoughts instantly can, if they so desire, delete their first message and try again for a more eloquent one.

If voice mail is not available, instructors might rig up an answering machine at a school phone, or they might use a home answering machine. This latter option might take some planning so that family members aren't disturbed by students calling at all hours of the day and night. Students could be given special times to call, and/or the volume on the phone and on the machine could be turned down at certain times. Whether this oral shaping of ideas takes place in class, in small groups or pairs in or out of class, or on a voice mail or answering machine system, the questions students address should help them formulate ideas related to the task at hand.

Teachers can design questions best suited to the particular project. If they have had past students complete a similar project, they can generate questions that will help writers better understand the assignment or prevent them from making the mistakes their predecessors made, such as not having an identifiable argument or not providing enough support. Having students formulate oral answers to specially designed questions forces them to actively focus on and generate ideas. Talking gets students engaged in the intellectual task in a way that hearing the teacher describe the assignment does not.

The theoretical base for this oral responding is the same one underlying freewriting, clustering, brainstorming, etc. It provides an opportunity for playing with ideas, using language—this time oral language—as an intellectual tool. For students whose primary way of knowing is speaking, oral outlining or previewing can make the difference between getting good ideas or being further frustrated by the slowness of written language. For students whose primary way of knowing is writing, oral outlining or previewing can challenge them to use less familiar paths to explore their memory. From a pragmatic standpoint, it saves time for students and teachers, it lightens the book bag load for both, and it saves paper.

For many of us writing teachers, the act of writing can trigger thoughts or connections we didn't have, or didn't know we had, before we started our written journal entry. This shaping-at-the-point-of-utterance triggering can also happen in oral journals, though it is more likely to happen if students do it off the cuff, without preparing a written script.

Oral Journal Example

Occasionally, I hear these connections happening in students' oral journals. One student in my rhetorical theory class, Derek, started his voice-mail response in a fairly conventional way, responding to a question I had asked this group to address regarding how what we were reading in our rhetorical theory class might connect with what they were doing in another class or in another aspect of their lives. He began by talking about another rhetoric class he was taking and also rhetoric's connection to technical writing, in which he had decided to specialize. Something in that context triggered something we had been discussing in class, invented or situated ethos, and its relation to his authority as a student to speak. Then he said, "Actually—something that just came to mind—" and proceeded to talk about how he was helping his brother write a letter to a professor requesting a grade change, or at least, that the professor agree to reconsider the grade on some assignments that fed into the final grade. Derek spoke at length about such issues as rhetorical situation, ethos, pathos, and other persuasive strategies he was discussing with his brother. Derek saw clear links between the rhetorical analyses we were doing in class and the rhetorical situations he was dealing with in "real life." He said this connection was "kinda cool."

Derek's voice-mail response is interesting in two ways. First, it demonstrates how talking, like writing, is a way of making knowledge. Like written language, spoken language can stimulate connections that the user did not have, at least consciously, at the beginning of the entry. We can hear that happening when the speaker says, "Actually, something that just came to mind." Second, Derek's response demonstrates the importance of "real life" tasks. What helped Derek relate one course to another, to see the relevance of what he was doing in his various classes, was when he faced the real-life task of helping his brother compose a letter that had important consequences regarding his brother's academic average.

Moving-to-Learn

Dancing is drawing the world.

—Paulo Freire[5]

Using kinesthetics to generate, organize, and develop ideas is underused in most English and writing classes. For some students, those with the kind of kinesthetic intelligence Howard Gardner describes, using movement as a way of knowing can help their writing by allowing them to use areas of intellectual strength to develop insights regarding textual organization and structure. And as with other approaches described in this book, using a non-linguistic pathway can challenge linguistically talented students by asking them to explore unfamiliar intellectual territory.

Thinking/Walking Through a Draft

As mentioned in Chapter 1, Karen Klein and Linda Hecker use kinesthetics to help students generate and organize their ideas through walking. In an approach Klein and Hecker devised called "walking the structure," students start in one section of a room and begin moving through it in ways that best represent the direction of their ideas: going forward to represent supportive information, standing still to represent getting stuck, or moving sideways to represent a different line of thought. They walk with another person, who jots down or records the walker's spoken ideas and physical directions. Typically, graphic symbols are used to represent physical directions taken (90–91). As Linda Hecker explains in a 1997 *English Journal* article, "movement can be used to facilitate learning instead of wasting everybody's energy by fighting against it" (47).

The point is to stimulate thinking in ways that are familiar for all students some of the time and unfamiliar for all students some of the time. Kinesthetic conceptualization will be comfortable for some and uncomfortable for others, in the same way writing is comfortable for some and uncomfortable for others. Working in a number of intellectual environments will provide the confidence writers need to move forward on a project, as well as the challenge needed to make it their best effort.

Tinkertoys

Linda Hecker at Landmark College has also written about using Tinkertoys. After reading about how Hecker used them, my colleague at Illinois State University, Anne Colloton, had an interesting experience using them in an undergraduate writing class. After her 15 students had completed and brought to class a first draft, she dumped several boxes of Tinkertoys on a big table in her computer-lab classroom. She explained that students were to use the toys to construct a model of their current draft. Students laughed at the prospect. No one made a move. Finally one student, a computer science major, went to the table and began working with the Tinkertoys. Other students looked on, curiously, and some began moving toward the table. Anne sensed that students felt awkward and silly with her watching them, so she left the room to let them work. Besides, since she was also doing the assignments in that class, she wanted to go into the hall to try the "walking the draft" exercise, described above, on her own draft, which she told me was very helpful. She read her paper out loud while she was walking, stimulating further ideas.

When she returned to the room, all fifteen students had models constructed and were explaining them to each other. Like Melissa and Terri, whose sketches sparked metaphors they later used in their revised papers, one of Anne's students, an art major, had a spindle in the center. He used the word "rotational" to describe his model. He later added that word to his revised paper in a description of an important concept. I have not yet used Tinkertoys in my classes, but Anne's experience convinces me that I should. In our discussion of how people work differently, Anne pointed out to me that in the film *A Few Good Men*, Tom Cruise walks around with a baseball bat, walking and talking and banging the bat. That's how that character gets ideas (Colloton 2000).

Peer Responding

Peer responding is well known in Composition Studies, though most people have mixed reactions to how well it "works." I discuss it here because of its multisensory nature, involving as it does reading, talking, writing, pointing, and sometimes cutting, pasting, and other structural movements. Although peer response is an inexact, sometimes frustrating process, if everyone takes it seriously, it can give insights to both writer and responder. In their metacognitive analyses of their projects, students often refer to the responding that they did and the responses they received. Some say that the peer responding was disappointing because people just said, "It was good," with no elaboration or productive critique. I think there will always be some students who do not take responding seriously.

Oral Peer Responses

Marie Ponsot and Rosemary Deen have suggested that listeners try to make their responses not "evaluations," but rather more neutral "observations." For example, a listener might observe: "The middle part is mostly dialogue." Another example of an observation they give is, "She says she is writing about *envy*. But I notice that the man who envied came up in only one sentence. All the rest was about the injured man" (1982, 59).

Dene Thomas and Gordon Thomas also recommend the use of declarative statements as useful responses to works in progress. Drawing on the work of psychologist Carl Rogers, they also recommend observation-like responses. Using what they call "Rogerian reflections," they encourage responders to begin sentences with the following phrases:

> What I hear you saying is . . .
>
> It seems like . . .
>
> It seems to me that . . .
>
> So . . .
>
> It sounds to me like you are trying to . . . (121)

In fact, their research on response and revision showed that "when a student gets nothing but questions, his or her answers get shorter, rather than longer"(120). This piece of information forced me to rethink the "facilitative questions" I had been routinely posing to students for years. Using Rogers' use of repetition as a model, Thomas and Thomas encourage responders to "reflect" what the writer seems to be saying, or to begin a conversation about the writing with a response such as, "Tell us what you're trying to do at this point, what you're writing about right now, in terms of writing" (120).

Writing center tutoring supports a similar approach. When writers produce an incomprehensible paragraph or sentence, being told the section is "awkward" is rightly seen as a negative response, and a useless one. Rather than rethink and rephrase the troublesome part, frustrated writers are just as likely to cross it out. Instead, listeners can draw on Elbow's concept of "movies of the mind" to explain how they heard the sentence. They can tell the story of how they read the piece, even to explain sentence-level problems: "I followed what you were saying up until that first comma, and then I got lost. Say in different words, out loud, what you meant by that last clause." If the listener can get the writer to articulate an idea that somehow became mangled in the written draft, the new sentence, shaped at the point of oral utterance, will almost always be more coherent and may even be written down for the revised version. Robert Parker and Vera Goodkin explain the role language, even, perhaps especially, informal language, plays in knowledge construction:

> Putting things in our own words, even in our most everyday, colloquial words, does not debase knowledge and thus is not something to be barely tolerated for "weaker" students, but a necessary step for each of us in the construction of knowledge. (3)

Peer interviewers can be taught how to make useful observations and statements, or, if they are particularly insecure about their roles as responders, they can also be given some basic, generic questions. When listening to a draft read aloud, students sometimes find they can concentrate better on listening if they do not have to generate questions. Therefore, sometimes writers, listeners, and teachers find it useful to have a list of questions already prepared that are appropriate for that stage of the particular writing project. The instructor and the students might together construct a list of questions designed to help novice responders get the conversation off the ground. Some questions can be fairly generic, useful for drafts of a number of assignments.

Generic questions for listeners to early drafts:

- As the writer was reading the draft, what part(s), if any, caught your attention? That is, what section(s) did you find yourself listening closely to? (If you found yourself dozing off in sections, the writer needs to know that, too.)

- What part(s) did you want to know more about? What else did you want to know?

Other questions may be more tailored to the specific task. For example, if the assignment is to write an argument or persuasive piece, the listener can help the writer determine if the text is clearly in that genre. If the writer is supposed to be simply summarizing or paraphrasing a reading, the listener can help pinpoint areas where the writer has crossed from summarizing into critique, for good or for ill. If the piece is supposed to be an analysis, a listener can help point out sections that are merely summary, a common problem in student writing from first-year through graduate school. Sometimes writers are the best generators of questions for their listeners and can simply be asked to generate questions to address in the interview:

- I used what I think is a great anecdote in the beginning of this piece, but I'm not sure readers will see the connection between the anecdote and the argument that follows. Do you see the connection? What is it? Should I leave it implied or spell it out?
- The sequence of this narrative is very clear to me. Could you follow the events, or do I need more transitions?
- The description of the lead dancer is very important to my review of the ballet. Could you picture her in detail? Do I need more description?
- How would you best characterize what you just listened to: (a) a list of facts; (b) an argument; (c) a narrative; (d) other? Explain.

Questions should be tailored to fit the project, and the responses to them may be jotted down or discussed orally. To keep the interview moving along, the questions could be written on a white board, overhead, computer screen, or scrap paper so the listener can refer to them later in the discussion. The point of this is to get writers talking at length about their ideas to help them use speech generatively. Listeners should use, adapt, or invent whatever questions they can in order to make that happen. It helps if students understand Britton's theory of writing, so that they understand the purpose of their questions.

Written Peer Responses

It is important that students receive a wide variety of written responses to their work-in-progress, as well as hear a discussion of it. Therefore, in my writing classes, when we are about midpoint in a major (ten- to twelve-page) project that takes about seven weeks to complete, I use the following cycle of response. Prior to a class meeting, several students will have e-mailed to me, and to everyone else in the class, a draft. On our own time outside of class, we all respond to that draft in a memo of about 250 words, which can also be forwarded to the entire class. Then during class time, we go around the room, with each responder reading or summarizing his or her memo. That way, everyone gets to hear a cross-section of response, and the writer also has a copy of all comments. Since the outside reading and responding to each draft takes at least a half hour, and since the class discussion of each draft takes time, I try to keep the responses limited to about three drafts per class meeting. Determining which writers send drafts on which days is decided by lottery. Then I put the schedule on a chart that's distributed several weeks in advance of the first due date. In a class of eighteen that meets twice a week, it takes about three weeks to complete this response cycle. Some students end up sending very early drafts, and some end up sending drafts when the project is almost due. Nevertheless, this draft-response cycle is well worth the time. For the most part, students seem to find giving and receiving responses useful.

> By reading my classmates' papers, I was more capable of seeing what I needed to work on as well. I found that many of the things I pointed out to them were also missing in my drafts. . . . To read, analyze, and critique others' drafts, it helped me practice what we were supposed to be doing in the project.—Melanie

> I found out some things also from responding to others' drafts that I tried to apply to my paper. I found that some papers were like mine and others had good ways of analyzing that I felt would be good in my paper (but I did not copy anybody). Overall, I felt that this paper was a good experience for me to realize that it is not always about analyzing what a person says, but how they say it.—Natalie

> Unlike any previous assignments, the assigned peer responses were tremendously helpful. Not only did my classmates' comments assist me in the construction of my paper; the responses that I gave to others turned me into being a better observer of rhetorical strategy. —Michelle

Terri said that the peer responses to her paper were not very helpful, first because few people responded and second because her draft was due early in the cycle and she had only a few pages written. However, what she did find helpful "were the many comments I was able to read on other people's drafts sent e-mail. Reading comments made to others made me think about if I had some of the same problems in my paper."

There are inevitably problems with this cycle of responding to drafts: hitches with e-mail accounts, a few students who don't fully participate, some people getting responses too early or too late to help them much. However, the overall effect of having everyone in the class respond in-depth to other people doing a similar project, and having them read or hear dozens of responses to their own or others' work, has a cumulative effect of making people very open to changing or even reconceiving their project. If nothing else, it makes them see that they're not the only ones struggling with this assignment, and by responding to others, they see they really do know what they're doing and can make insightful, analytic comments. As Freire and others have shown us, confidence and security have much to do with writing. Here we see how peer responses helped Leah overcome her insecurity about this project:

When it came time to write my draft, I was able to come up with things to say but that's where my insecurity came. Because of being unsure if I was doing what needed to be accomplished in this paper, I only analyzed one letter. After getting comments I felt a little bit better but just let my paper sit for a while without looking at it. Now after giving more comments to classmates and reading more papers I will be able to continue to finish my paper.—Leah

Peer responding makes students more alert readers and more productively critical of their own work. They become more confident, even as they are challenged, because they see that others are struggling with problems similar to theirs. They are also able to see an angle of analysis someone else used: focusing on a writer's metaphors, for example, or on use of passive voice, or pathetic appeals or citations from respected journals. This opens more angles of analysis in their own project. They stop talking about whether they'll "have enough information," a worry they hyperventilate about when they first begin this project, and they begin to plan what sections of their analysis they'll need to cut.

This transformation takes time, and it doesn't happen for everyone at the same moment. We work on this project for approximately seven weeks, during which time students search for letters to analyze, and read rhetorical analyses by published rhetoricians and by past students in the class. They begin their drafts and they respond to four or five drafts per week. We give our responses orally in class, and writers get a copy either via e-mail or by printout. The process is not a painless one. People become frustrated, overwhelmed, confused, and panicky before they begin to make some claims about the texts they are analyzing.

How is this kind of responding multisensory? First, the responses are heard by everyone. We go around the room and responders read or talk from their written response to the writer. The writer also gets the written response via e-mail. Each person both gives and receives responses, so they write, read, speak, and listen many times throughout the cycle. When they hear praise or questions about someone else's draft, they consider how those comments might apply to their project. Even though all these responses are also written, it is worth the class time to discuss them because hearing the responses reinforces the overall emphasis on what people are doing well, and what most people need to work on further. Having this conversation every day also reinforces students' authority as insightful readers who can also use that authority as readers and writers of their own text. So while this oral give-and-take is not multisensory in the same way working with Tinkertoys is, it provides multiple-perspective experiences for students, giving them a different lens through which to view their own draft when they return to it.

Spatial Insights

This responding cycle also causes spatial changes in students' drafts. When they send their e-mailed drafts to the entire class, the text is interrupted in different ways. For example, I often respond to e-mailed drafts by hitting "Reply." When I see a section I want to respond to, I hit the return key, scroll down the draft, and insert my comments after a particular word or sentence or section of analysis. I usually use a different font or at least skip spaces, so my comments are easier to read. Then I electronically copy my comments to the whole class, as do the peer responders.

Other responders sometimes model this responding format, the result being that the writer gets five or six e-mailed responses with his or her text broken up in different ways, with blocks of inserted questions, suggestions, or advice to move or delete. It becomes more difficult to think of the draft as an untouchable monolith and easier to think of it as chunks that can be expanded, moved, or jettisoned. Many people say at the end of this project that they have never before done as much deep revising as they did on this paper. Robert said, "Personally, I got a lot of good feedback that caused me to cut and paste my paper to bits." In addition, the substantial responding they do to the drafts of others working on a project similar to theirs gives them a valuable reader-identified perspective when they come back to their own drafts. As Richard Beach points out, this kind of responding helps writers "adopt a reader's perspective, necessary for distancing themselves from their text" (1989, 139).

At what point in the cycle of getting and receiving responses this change happens would be difficult to pinpoint, and what exactly changes would be difficult to quantify. It's more a gradual change in perspective that allows writers to see their texts as readers might. They become more alert to what might confuse those who do not have access to what is inside a writer's head. When writers realize their peers are confused by sections of their papers, they revise to make their drafts more reader-friendly.

Social Intelligence

Finally, this cycle of responding, whether oral or written, taps into a student's social intelligence. Effective responders need both insight and tact, a delicate balance of straightforwardness and compassion, praise and productive critique. What's more, responders must figure out which of their classmates need different proportions of each. Who does well with this social savvy is sometimes surprising. As the weeks go by, students begin to look to certain people for additional feedback, those who rightly see this as a compliment. These responders are invariably generous with their comments, which are by now voluntary, and their extra concentration on other people's drafts is usually rewarded when they revise their own drafts, because they have seen such a variety of approaches.

Peer Interviewing Strategies

In the organizational stages of writing, the peer interview, with writers speaking and listening, provides an oral give-and-take that can spark insights, connections, and examples that writers might not generate on their own, working with the written draft alone. Peer interviewing is not a new idea. It has long been a part of conventional process pedagogy and writing-center peer-tutoring strategies. However, it can take practice before students get good at it. They begin with the expectation that the best revising advice comes from the teacher. Natalie said, "I weighed the teacher response more heavily and tried to make the most changes from what advice I got [from her]." And of course, since teachers are the ones who usually grade the papers, the student is sensible to seek his or her input. But because of this, students may be predisposed to think peer input is useless.

Writing centers have long used successfully the practice of having tutors listen to a draft read aloud by the writer. There is, however, a "teacher/student" paradigm that exists even in "peer tutoring" situations that writing centers cannot help but create: the tutor represents authority. Peer interviewing in a class between paired classmates, however, virtually eliminates that hierarchical situation. In a classroom, where in a few moments the writer will become the listener and vice versa, students are truly peers. This peer dynamic allows the text and its revision possibilities to be foregrounded, not the power difference between two people. Peer interviewing, besides reinforcing the writer's role as *writer* (as opposed to *student*), promotes the writer's speaking skills as well as the partner's listening skills. Writing, speaking, and listening are all taken seriously, with both partners pooling all their talents and skills to the mutual benefit of both.

Here are some ways peer interviewing can work. On a preassigned day, writers bring in a draft or even a preliminary outline or sketch of their project idea. In a computer lab, they might simply call it up on a screen. In pairs, they take turns reading their drafts, out loud, to their partner. The partners are given instructions to listen carefully to the draft, and to ask to hear it read more than once if necessary. By listening to, rather than reading, the text, peer responders are forced to concentrate on the *ideas* in the draft, rather than on surface issues of punctuation and spelling. The listeners are told to ask questions about the piece they just heard, especially open-ended questions "to get the writer talking."

To model this process, I sometimes ask for one "brave soul" to read his or her draft out loud to the class, while I listen closely, sometimes asking for a second reading, and then posing some open-ended questions. There is no need to prepare questions ahead of time. I want to convince students that the questions will spring to mind naturally after having heard the draft, and they always do.

- You said you were scared on your first day at the university. What was it like when you went to your first class?
- What one thing scared you the most?
- You said you now feel more comfortable here. Tell me more about that one moment that was a turning point in your attitude toward this school.

Open-ended questions or directions like these will get writers talking their way through ideas still inchoate in their drafts. Listeners do not need formal training in composition theory to pay close attention to the draft being read to them. If they are initially given some basic questions to pose, both reader and listener can worry less about "criticism" and use their energies to focus on ideas. Listeners are not to "correct" or "praise," but simply to ask questions. I tell listeners to act like good talk show hosts, questioning their guests about subjects that come up, asking for more details, responding to strong opinions, etc.

I then instruct writers and/or listeners to jot down ideas that came up in this discussion that a writer might want to explore further in a subsequent draft. The listener's point-of-entry will tell writers much about the most compelling part of their draft. They can immediately see the effect of their writing on another human being, a person whose job is not to "correct" the draft, but to engage the ideas in it.

These peer interviews are also an effective way to pull novice writers out of the praise/correction model in which their own writing experience may have been steeped. In other words, when students are asked to respond to a piece of writing, they often think their job is to "fix" it. If told to respond, not correct, they may automatically think they are instead only to "praise" what they read, or troll for spelling errors. This approve/disapprove binary is partly due to our culture's knee-jerk urge to binarize everything. However, it intimidates both reader and responder, interfering with the concentration needed to use the time productively, to help the writer discover meaning through speaking.

How does reading out loud to a peer group for their oral responses relate to the power issues raised earlier? How does it fit into the consensus/discensus issues debated by Rorty, Bruffee, Myers, and Trimbur and discussed in the Introduction? It provides another example of contraries. It's true that consensus in the groups may play a part in reinstating the status quo, Rorty's abnormal discourse notwithstanding. Students must conform to academic conventions whether this is pointed out to them by their teachers or their peers. However, when peer response works well, several things happen.

First of all, because more students tend to participate in this process than they might in a conventional class with the teacher lecturing or leading the discussion, students get to see different people contributing, and different intellectual strengths at work. It is often surprising in these oral exercises to see who does and does not have impressive insight on a draft, who can articulate an insight, who can do so both candidly and kindly, with some well-placed humor. It changes the dynamic of the class by tapping into different talent veins. This kind of oral peer review may be critiqued by those who say it doesn't really challenge hegemonic economic systems. But on a local level, it challenges the commonplace that teachers hold all the knowledge about revising a text, and it challenges classroom assumptions about which students are "smart." This classroom activity does not change the world. But it chips away damaging pieces of it.

The oral, graphic, and kinesthetic approaches in this chapter to generating and organizing ideas provide the kind of intellectual play Vygotsky argued was crucial to higher-level learning. The next chapter suggests ways these approaches can help students revise and edit later-stage drafts.

Notes

1. One of the manuscript reviewers called a version of this activity "mystery pot," a term I had not heard before. He or she did not give a reference, so I was unable to determine if that activity is similar to the one I describe here.

2. One easy way to make these cards is to type them up in a format similar to Figure 3–1, using a word processor. Then have the resulting printed sheet(s) photocopied onto paperboard, which can then be cut into "cards" and rubber banded together for as many groups as needed.

3. I am grateful to Abigail Waldron for making me more sensitive to the role Venn diagrams can play in conceptualization. I met her on a CCCC 2000 panel, where we were both presenters.

4. For a fuller explanation of oral journal use, see my "Oral Journals: Voice Mail and Tape Recorders as Inclusive and Challenging Forums," *The Journal Book for Teachers of At-Risk College Writers.* eds. Susan Gardner and Toby Fulwiler, 116–28. Portsmouth, NH: Boynton/Cook, 1999.

5. *Convergence* 6 (1) (1973): 81.

Chapter Four

Revising and Editing
Myths, Metaphors,
and Multisensory Strategies

Usage can be defined neutrally as the customary ways in which things are done in written discourse. A more biased and yet more accurate definition is this: usage rules are the conventions of written English that allow Americans to discriminate against one another. Questions of usage are tied to social attitudes about who is intelligent and well-educated, and who is not.

—Sharon Crowley
and Deborah Hawhee[1]

I begin this chapter with a sigh. With contradictions chattering in my head. Grammar is important. No it isn't. Yes it is, but not in the way most people think. It's oppressive and useless to "teach" it. It's oppressive to think we can just ignore it. Some people just "get" it. Some people don't. It's a minor issue. It's a major issue. Our colleagues think it's our job to "teach grammar." What do they really mean when they say that? How can I help my students, my colleagues, and my contemporaries in the general public to see all the arguments about grammar, the complexities of its controversies, before I begin to give advice about issues of grammar? How can I even step far enough away from it myself to get a useful overview? The problem is, "grammar" becomes an issue instantly, even as I type this "freewrite" to get me into this chapter. I just went back and corrected "away" because I initially typed "awry"—a subliminal message, perhaps, that I should not correct but expand. So that's just one small issue—the kind of interruptions Peter Elbow points out that people constantly make as they write. Did I lose a priceless gem of thought as I went back and corrected the typo? Probably not. But you never know. I do have suggestions for using multisensory strategies to address issues of grammar. But first some sighs, some disclaimers, some overviews, and some contradictions.

There are many reasons for what Crowley and Hawhee have called "Americans' obsession with correctness and clarity" (1999, 263), only some of which will be explored here. Any venturing into revising and editing territories is bound to be selective, incomplete, and controversial, confronting as it must old but ongoing debates about grammar, process pedagogy, and direct versus indirect instruction. However, decisions about how, when, or whether to help students revise and edit are complex ones, inextricably related to conscious or unconscious assumptions about language and learning. Many of the theoretical and practical problems discussed here may be considered to be long-buried by some. I exhume them here first to argue that the very complexity of these issues prevents them from being resolved once and for all, and, further, that their vexing refusal to stay buried can invigorate our pedagogies by forcing us to re-visit and re-articulate the reasons we do what we do (or don't do). As Paulo Freire understood, uncertainties demand rethinkings. In other words, instead of groaning when yet another voice laments our students' perceived lack of grammar or our perceived refusal to teach it, we should embrace these ghosts for the opportunity they provide to debate with them (and again with ourselves) the conundrums these issues present.

Cleaning out the Closet

To switch the metaphor yet again: When we clean our revising and editing closet, we should put all our research and ideologies on the bed as we might our clothes, sorting through the treasured heirlooms, the cheap fads, and the hand-me-downs, before we add our new sneakers. This sorting involves both embarrassing and pleasurable rediscoveries, as well as some painful decisions. The more often we do it, the better.

Furthermore, dragging one thing out of the closet can sometimes bring other things tumbling down on our heads. These tangential oddities interrupt our sorting and invite us to examine the T-shirt from Alaska, the yellow gingham draft doggie, or the letter stashed in the corner behind the tap shoes. Likewise, reopening the grammar closet forces us to examine what lurks behind our public stance on revising, editing, and "correctness."

We must interrogate our assumptions and try to understand what we're doing and why, what a well-edited piece of writing does and does not indicate, why "correctness" is neither simple nor ideologically neutral, but associated in powerful ways to ethos, class status, and social constructions of taste and even morality. We must reexamine—and help our students see—how perceived correctness in writing is like perceived correctness in wardrobe style, related more to context than to stable rules.

Difficult Decisions About What Comes out of the Closet: Process Pedagogy

A good place to begin this complex discussion about revising, editing, and how or whether to teach writing conventions, is with Lisa D. Delpit's candid, controversial critique of process pedagogy that appeared in the August 1988 *Harvard Educational Review*. In her essay, Delpit rightly argued that classrooms and writing pedagogies are about issues of power, and that some students already have, because of their middle- or upper-class social class status, "more accoutrements of the culture of power already in place" than those from a lower social class (285). Among these accoutrements are internalized rules about academic behavior, from how to dress to how to adhere to constructed grammar and usage conventions. In order to be successful, Delpit argues, students must already have, or learn, these conventions. She further argues that explicit teaching is the best way for them to learn.

In Keith Gilyard's 1996 critique of Delpit's article, he tells us that he deliberately uses the past tense to summarize her argument because, he says, "I don't presume she holds those exact views today." He also presents her views in the past tense in order to "stress my use of them as historical reference points that merely tip an iceberg of contemporary dialectics about writing-process pedagogy" (1996a, 90). It's also clear that by "dispens[ing] with the academic convention of writing about her texts in the present tense," Gilyard is also subtly pointing out the constructed nature of that convention regarding verb tense, even as he takes issue with and expands that convention. In my continued summary of Delpit, I follow Gilyard's lead and deliberately use past tense.

Delpit argued that using process pedagogy for revising and editing matters, with its emphasis on peer group response (as opposed to directive teacher commentary), leaves too much for students to figure out indirectly. It relies on an osmosis that might never occur, leaving students who come to class without power still searching at the end of the class for the "cultural capital" that their classmates come already possessing. "If you are not already a participant in the culture of power, being told explicitly the rules of that culture makes acquiring power easier" (283). This difference in pedagogical approaches is related to issues of revising and editing because it has to do with perceived issues of "grammar," "correctness," "usage," and the like.

Delpit was critiquing a process pedagogy of discovery (or an interpretation of one) that was popular in the 1980s, a representation of which can be seen in Lil Brannon's and Gordon Pradl's "The Socialization of Writing Teachers," which appeared in *The Journal of Basic Writing* in 1984:

> Teachers do not have knowledge to impart, nor do they hold the answers to how the writing can be improved. Only the writers can discover new ways of clarifying their meanings, and this discovery can be quickened and enhanced by the questioning reader. Teachers, then, are collaborators, readers among a group of readers, persons who reflect back to the writer what they have heard, what they expect to hear, what they wish to know more about. They are not authoritarians, guardians of standard written English, correctors of essays but participants in a community of writers, taking a stance which reinforces both teacher's and students' writing groups. (36–37)

Criticizing extreme forms of pedagogies that assume students will implicitly figure out codes and rules of writing and academia as they become immersed in both, Delpit maintained that students from "non-middle-class homes" should be told explicitly what is expected in school and in writing, which reflects middle- and upper-class cultural assumptions in ways that are often invisible. To illustrate her point, she used the following anecdote:

> When I lived in several Papua New Guinea villages for extended periods to collect data, and when I go to Alaskan villages for work with Alaskan Native communities, I have found it unquestionably easier—psychologically and pragmatically—when some kind soul has directly informed me about such matters as appropriate dress, interactional styles, embedded meanings, and taboo words or actions. I contend that it is much the same for anyone seeking to learn the rules of the culture of power. Unless one has had the leisure of a lifetime of "immersion" to learn them, explicit presentation makes learning immeasurably easier. (283)

In addressing the controversy that Delpit's article ignited, Gilyard observes that in spite of its title, "The Silenced Dialogue: Power and

Pedagogy in Educating Other People's Children," this piece had the ironic effect of silencing "much of the audience she was imploring to speak" (87). He said many white teachers felt they could not defend process writing because "Delpit had played the so-called race card, positing a variation of the basic argument 'I'm Black, so I know what's best for Black kids'" (89). Gilyard critiques Delpit for not providing details of the bad instruction she cites as evidence for her views. He argues that "specifying the tenets of such instruction" would re-open and keep open a necessary discussion of process pedagogy and its appropriateness for all students (89). Toward that end, Gilyard further critiques Delpit for "unnecessary binarism and reductionism" in her depiction of process writing. Drawing on Steven Zemelman's and Harvey Daniels' list of fifteen qualities that characterize process writing, Gilyard provides a richer, more complete description of it (90–91). He also agrees with Zemelman and Daniels that "it is profoundly, dangerously, insidiously wrong" (1993, 355) to think we will find one "right way" to teach every child (Gilyard 1996a, 91). One of my reasons for selecting the Delpit/Gilyard essay pair is to draw attention to the need for ongoing examinations of complex issues and the need to avoid a search for one answer.

Although Gilyard initially critiques what he sees as Delpit's narrow conception and rejection of process writing pedagogy, he ultimately calls brilliant her analysis of the real issue underlying this controversy about teaching. That real issue is "the culture of power" (94). Gilyard agrees with Delpit about "the need to explicitly teach African American students the linguistic and cultural codes that may enable more effective participation by them in the wider realms of language and power" (94).

When we clean out the revising/editing closet, what should hit us on the head is the role power plays in what we usually think of as "minor" issues. As Delpit put it: "Those with power are frequently the least aware of—or least willing to acknowledge—its existence. Those with less power are often most aware of its existence" (283). To paraphrase Delpit, "grammar" issues are minor only to those for whom it is not an issue.

In *Defending Access*, Tom Fox raises a more ominous possibility about issues of power. He says debates about language "standards" are not really about neutral questions of literacy: "I want to argue specifically and strongly against the narrow view that the crisis of access is caused mainly by underpreparation or a lack of literacy skills on the part of students of color" (10).

As we shall see, in further discussions in this chapter about revising and editing, many controversies that seem to be about "minor" issues of grammar, punctuation, syntax, usage, and "surface correctness," are really about power: who has it, who doesn't, who wants it, who likes to flaunt it, who may not want to share it, and who may prefer to disguise it as simply an issue of "correctness."

Wardrobe as Code for Intelligence

When we clean out our closets, we not only sort the cool clothes from the absurd ones, we get a sense of our histories: why we thought we could wear such a thing ten years ago, and why we must use it today as a dust rag. We may also rethink the role clothing plays in society, a role also related to power, as well as who stands to gain or lose by the unspoken societal codes that clothing represents. Whose interests are served by the style and comfort level of this clothing? What do we gain and lose by adhering to its unspoken codes? As Gilyard, Delpit, and Fox argue implicitly, we need to ask similar questions about the societal codes that support our stance toward writing style and comfort level, revising and editing, standards and correctness.

Our literacy-loving society has unspoken codes about surface correctness; that is, having one's spelling, punctuation, and usage ducks in a row, something that students no doubt know intuitively. But these unspoken codes and assumptions should be voiced so that they can be accounted for or challenged. Unfortunately, readers often link surface correctness with "good writing," which they then link with "good taste," or at least taste perceived to be good, even higher on a moral scale, by those in the privileged class. They also link "good writing" with intelligence.

The assumptions linking surface correctness with intelligence are perhaps so pervasive that they are invisible. But there are indicators: Students who make the most surface errors (in the form of breaches of usage, grammar, spelling, or punctuation conventions) end up in the lowest-track writing classes, as if spelling and punctuation errors were the footprints of inadequate thinking. There are indicators in the way too many of us meet the "They can't-even-write-a-complete-sentence!" mantras of our colleagues with shaking heads and post-lapsarian laments. There are indicators in the way students' malapropisms are collected and posted on office doors or gleefully forwarded through e-mail and listservs, as if proof of students' stupidity and professors' superiority. As Crowley and Hawhee have pointed out, this linking of literacy and intelligence was not always thus: "Ancient rhetoricians would be very surprised by the modern association of intelligence and education with literacy—the ability to read and write" (275). In *Composition in the*

University, Crowley shows how contemporary assumptions about "correctness" and intelligence are not new. She cites Brainerd Kellogg's 1893 view that

> one's English is already taken as the test and measure of his culture—he is known by the English he keeps. To mistake his words (even to mispronounce them or to speak them indistinctly), to huddle them as a mob into sentences, *to trample on plain rules of grammar, to disregard the idioms of the language,—these things, all or severally, disclose the speaker's intellectual standing.* One's English betrays his breeding, tells what society he frequents, and determines what doors are open to him or be closed against him. (my emphasis; 63)

Even in late-20th century articles, it is not difficult to find this presumed association between surface features of a text and its writer's intelligence. In 1981, Stephen P. Witte and Lester Faigley analyzed the textual features of high-rated and low-rated student essays, summarizing and commenting on the findings. Among other things, Witte and Faigley found that the low-rated essays exhibited a limited vocabulary, which was inadequate for writers to expand or give examples of ideas in their papers. Although they wonder whether a writer's invention skills may be related to vocabulary "in ways yet unexplored" (198), Witte and Faigley go on to assume that a person's vocabulary as evident in a written text can be taken as evidence of that person's complete vocabulary: "If students do not have in their working vocabularies the lexical items required to extend, explore, or elaborate the concepts they introduce, practice in invention can only have a limited effect on overall writing quality" (198). While Witte and Faigley may be right that a sophisticated vocabulary helps people add the "lexical collocations" (elaborations and examples) that were valued by readers when they separated the high- from the low-rated essays, they should consider the possibility that for some students, writing does *not* provide the best opportunity to show working vocabularies or collocations.

As writing center tutors often discover, a student who has trouble *writing* about ideas may be able to *speak* about them at length when questioned orally. It may very well be that for Compositionists, writing *is* the best vehicle for showing off what we know. But we cannot assume that is the case for everyone. There could be other reasons a student's writing does not display a sophisticated vocabulary, for example. One possibility is that the student does know other words, but is so afraid of misspelling them that she sticks with simpler words. She may have been asked to produce the writing quickly and did not have the time needed to recall the terms she knows but cannot quickly remember. She may have to move around or to talk through her ideas before she has access to the words she wants. Or she may occasionally confuse them with other words, producing the malapropisms that too many of her friends, relatives, or teachers have taken delight in pointing out. She has learned too well how wrong words or misspelled ones will be received by her readers, how they will judge her intelligence by them, so she does not take the risk of using any but the most mundane words, the ones she'll recall, use correctly, and spell right. Or, she uses a thesaurus, and retrieves the perfect word—but not for the particular sentence at hand—and her work announces its author as a barbarian at the gate.

As Composition instructors, we are invested in writing. We see it as an intellectual tool because it functions like one reliably for us most of the time. But we should not see writing as an automatic gauge of every student's thinking process, any more than we would want our thinking processes judged by how well we solve a calculus problem, drive the streets of Boston, or do a cartwheel.

The Thesaurus as Bad Fashion Consultant

In my past work as a writing center tutor and then director, I have advised many students not to use a thesaurus. They use one, they tell me, because they know that a sophisticated vocabulary is valued by readers, or because someone has told them not to repeat the same word throughout an essay. When they turn to a thesaurus for a synonym, they often pick a word they recognize, but have never used before in a sentence. The result is often a sentence faux pas, which backfires on the writer, drawing attention not to her skills as a sophisticated language user but as an amateur open to ridicule. The line here is a narrow, cruel one. "Big words" used right say one thing about a writer; used wrong they announce that she is not in the club, like shining a spotlight on a ripped seam or the cheese dribbled on a shirt.

To help such students tap into ways to further develop their work, I try to get them talking about their project. If we run out of time, I advise them to talk or argue about the issue with a roommate or friend, to get their thoughts activated and to write down or record what came to mind. There are now reasonably priced computer-chip recorders that store voice notes without audio tapes. If we do have time during the session to talk, students usually come up with much to add to their draft, in language that is both sophisticated and familiar to them. What strikes me is how well students have learned society's lesson about vocabulary level, word use, written language, and intelligence. They are wise to be afraid of writing. It's no wonder that they hate it.

As writing teachers, we forget how much we know, how much we've read, how comfortable we are, most of the time, with written language. We forget how routine, if not easy, it is for us to analyze who will be reading our text, to think about ways we can appeal, rhetorically, to that audience. We forget the confidence we have (mostly) in beginning a writing project, struggling with it, even as we know it's going to be a struggle, re-working it again and again as we negotiate our own or our readers' critiques. We finish the thing, or at least we stop working on it. We send it off in an envelope, or we press "Send." We know how it feels to have finished many, many writing projects, more or less successfully. And yet even we, who have had years of successful writing and revising experience, have doubts and fears. How many times as I worked on this project have I painted my toenails, pored over grocery store flyers, watered the already sodden plants, checked the mail, stared at the fish tank, or even made the bed—anything to avoid sitting back down at the computer? Why? I think because I'm afraid. Afraid I'll have a writer's block. Afraid that I won't. Afraid of what I won't write. Afraid of what I will. If I, who have many years of mostly good memories of writing behind me, have such terrors of writing, what terrors must haunt my students, especially those whose drafts are so full of ripped seams and cheese dribbles?

Outward Appearances, Wardrobe Faux Pas, and Taste

In his well-known 1981 *CCC* essay, "The Phenomenology of Error," Joseph Williams wonders why usage choices such as "irregardless" and "hopefully" are judged with such "unusual ferocity" and seen as "horrible atrocities" (152). Williams goes on to point out "errors" in the very handbooks that warn about them. He makes the vivid point that readers "find" errors in those texts in which they expect to find them (i.e., ones written by students), but they do not look for, and therefore do not see, errors in texts where they do not expect to find them (i.e., grammar handbooks). His point is that "error" is a phenomenon of context, a matter of who is reading whose writing for what purpose.

Early on in his essay, Williams discusses common grammar and usage errors and argues that they are like social gaffes in some ways, but unlike them in that they do not violate personal or psychic space in the way that "defective social behavior" does, such as spilling coffee on someone or telling a racist joke. He wonders "why so much heat is invested in condemning a violation whose consequence impinges not at all on our personal space?" (153). "But no matter how 'atrocious' or 'horrible' or 'illiterate' we think an error like *irregardless* or a *like* for an *as* might be, it does not jolt my ear in the same way an elbow might" (153).

However, it might be argued that the minor linguistic "errors" Williams describes *do* violate the personal space of some readers in ways that have to do with social class and taste. Williams comes close to saying as much when he points out that the degree of hostility with which those errors are greeted must be due to "deep psychic forces" we do not completely understand. These "errors," minor though they are, are the leisure suits of language use: instant signs of social class and education, ways to determine who belongs to the club and who does not. In ways readers might not consciously realize, a writer who uses "irregardless" or "between you and I" might be viewed as an interloper who must be stopped at the door, a crasher of an academic party, like a female professor wearing a sunflower-print tent dress to a job interview. The word choices and kinds of errors people make are bullhorns announcing that they haven't been to the right dinner parties, read the right journals, or avoided the right theme parks.

As Sharon Crowley points out, our views of taste stem from 18th-century European notions of it as something that a person is either born with or not, yet also something that 19th-century rhetoric texts nevertheless attempted to teach (1995, 12–13). Her anecdote about food preference is a wonderful way to explain language use as an issue of learned taste. On a road trip through the Midwest, she was reminded that her current taste for "espresso coffee and olive oil" was acquired during her years of living in the West, just as a penchant for "orange Jell-O salad with carrots inside and mayonnaise on top" is a learned taste in another part of the country (11).

Tracing traditions of taste through Alexander Pope, David Hume, and Immanuel Kant in the eighteenth-century and then focusing on Hugh Blair and the influence his work had on the nineteenth-century "pedagogy of taste," Crowley argues that taste functions primarily to discriminate and exclude: "The pedagogy of taste helps students to internalize a set of rules that mark their inclusion in bourgeois subjectivity at the same time it sets them off from members of other classes" (18). Crowley goes on to argue that the mandatory first-year composition course of today is also implicated in "the maintenance and promulgation of bourgeois subjectivity," and that students in those courses who are not from upper or middle classes "will find their differences continually remarked by such instruction" (19).

Crowley's point here indirectly answers Joseph Williams' musing above regarding why a certain grammar and usage "violation" (such as "irregardless") is met with such "ferocity" when it does not violate our personal space. Nor does it make the sentence less clear. What it does make more clear, however, is the writer's social or educational class, which may cause some readers to see it as a more alarming violation: of one social class attempting to impinge on the personal space, or cultural capital, of another. So the middle- or upper-class reader delights in seeking out and exposing the tiniest departures from linguistic conventions, but only, as Williams points out, if they come from those outside the circle, such as students. Insiders and perceived authorities, such as handbook writers, can make the same departures and they are literally not even noticed.

Citing reader-response theory, C. H. Knoblauch and Lil Brannon also point out that readers' conception of the authority of a writer impacts how they perceive his or her text. Further, when given the authority to evaluate a text, readers will readily do so, usually negatively, and they will typically "cite any idiosyncrasy of form or technique, idea or style, any authorial choice that challenges their personal preferences, as an 'error'" (1984, 161). What's more, Tom Fox argues that "errors" in language use are inevitably linked with moral flaws: "Literacy studies in the last ten years have effectively demonstrated that what gets called illiterate is historically and socially contingent and that the charge of illiteracy carries with it a potent charge of moral unfitness" (43).

"Proper" English as Ticket to Ride

Whether "proper English" can get an outsider into privileged circles is itself debatable. Richard Rodriguez believes that English is the ticket to participation in mainstream American culture (*Hunger of Memory*). Victor Villanueva (1987) takes issue with Rodriguez's view that in spite of the sacrifices in lost culture a child makes when he or she learns "Anglais," the benefits of acceptance outweigh the loss in cultural separation from family and home community. Villanueva argues that discrimination in the United States involves more than the niceties of language used by the people being discriminated against. He makes a distinction between a group he calls "immigrants," who *chose* to come to the United States (or whose ancestors did), and a group he calls "minorities," people in the United States whose ancestors were colonized or enslaved. Villanueva points out that "some ethnic minorities have not been assimilated in the way the Ellis Islanders were" (18) and he uses an analogy about food to illustrate this difference:

> Who speaks of a German-American sausage, for instance? It's a hot dog. Yet tacos remain ethnic, sold under a mock Spanish mission bell or a sombrero. You will find refried beans under "ethnic foods"

in the supermarket, not among other canned beans, though items as foreign-sounding as sauerkraut are simply canned vegetables. Mexican foods, even when as Americanized as the taco salad or Mexican-Velveeta, remain distinctly Mexican. (18)

With another anecdote, Villanueva continues his objection to the commonplace of "proper English" as ticket to ride, this one about his father searching for an apartment in uptown New York. When the landlord heard Villanueva's father using "the sounds of a Spanish speaker attempting his best English," there were no vacancies. However, when his father said the family was from Spain, there was suddenly an opening. The initial pronouncement of "no vacancy" Villanueva thinks was due to stereotypical views of Puerto Ricans. The sudden opening was due to the instant transformation, in the landlord's eyes, of Villanueva's father from "minority" to "immigrant." As Villanueva puts it: "The immigrant could enter where the minority could not. My father's English hadn't improved in the five minutes it had taken for the situation to change" (20). Many students struggle to improve their writing, believing "good English" is the key to success. To a certain extent, this belief is supported. However, students should be privy to socioeconomic factors quietly manipulating people's reactions to other people—because of, or in spite of, their language use.

Myths About the "Grammar" Wardrobe

In a 1985 *College English* article, Patrick Hartwell summarizes the previous seventy-five years' worth of grammar research and debate, especially Braddocks', Lloyd-Jones', and Schoer's 1963 study showing the uselessness of direct formal grammar instruction.[2] Hartwell also shows how suspicion of such research, as well as rehearsals of recurring "literacy crises," are the forces that re-ignite grammar debates, causing all discussions of "grammar," to begin, once again, at the beginning. Hartwell highlights studies that suggest direct grammar teaching, which he sees as "embedded in larger models of the transmission of literacy" (108), has little effect on the quality of student writing. He says that people interpret research the way they want to and that more experimental research will not resolve the debate (106–107).

Drawing on W. Nelson Francis' 1954 distinction among "three meanings of grammar," Hartwell adds two more, for a total of five:

- Grammar 1 is the internalized grammatical rules that enable even two-year-olds to speak in grammatically correct sentences, having no formal knowledge of the names of the structures being used.

Hartwell calls this "the grammar in our heads" (111), though I want to return later to Hartwell's use of "our" and the assumptions he seems to be making about who "we" are.

- Grammar 2 is linguistics, the formal study of patterns.

- Grammar 3 is what W. Nelson Francis called "linguistic etiquette"; Hartwell calls it "usage" and acknowledges Joseph Williams' problematizing of how usage is wielded in our society (see above). Using more direct language, Sharon Crowley and Debra Hawhee define usage as "the conventions of written English that allow Americans to discriminate against one another" (1999, 283).

- Grammar 4 is one of Hartwell's subdivisions of Grammar 2, which he calls "American structuralist grammar" or "the grammars used in the schools" (1985, 110). Here Hartwell cites Charlton Laird's description of this grammar as "the grammar of Latin, ingeniously warped to suggest English" (1970, 294). Crowley and Hawhee also point out that traditional grammar teaching sometimes imposes Latin rules on English, for example the "rule" against split infinitives, which made sense in Latin, but not in English (283).

- Grammar 5 is another division of Grammar 2, which is "grammatical terms used in the interest of teaching prose style." These terms vary, Hartwell argues, depending on the handbook used to teach them (110).

Hartwell's lengthy description of the five "grammars" gives names to various complexities of this issue, making it easier to talk about with students or with interested members of the academic or public community. The following statement from his article is a lucid summary of his position:

> Thus if we think seriously about error and its relationship to the worship of formal grammar study, we need to attempt some massive dislocation of our traditional thinking, to shuck off our hyperliterate perception of the conscious knowledge that our theory of language gives us. (Hartwell 1985, 121)

His comments here and above ("the grammar in our head") about "our" raises questions about who "we" are. Does everyone have the same internalized structure of English? Do all children internalize those structures in the same way and at the same time? Can implicit learning be enhanced for some students by selected explicit learning or teaching? As Lisa Delpit has suggested, these are questions that have not been fully explored. Hartwell is probably right that more experimental research will no doubt be designed, carried out, and interpreted according to people's preexisting assumptions (conscious or unconscious) about language and grammar, and will therefore not answer questions once and for all. However, as Composition instructors who have spent much of our time and intellectual energy focused on language and issues of language, we need to take care not to assume that our ease and pleasure with written language will be the same for all our students, if only they become engaged with critical social issues. We must ask who is speaking when talking about "*our* theory of language," and "the grammar in *our* heads" (my emphasis). We must examine those phrases for their assumed universality.

In spite of, or perhaps because of, questions that need to be raised here, Hartwell's article is a good base from which to "begin at the beginning." His essay would be an appropriate common text for these discussions because, unlike many academic arguments, Hartwell's research is drawn from a variety of disciplines: reading, experimental psychology, linguistics, and teaching English as a second language. As I have argued elsewhere, we need to expand our research circle into other fields, even more than we currently do—not to find answers, but to ask more sophisticated questions about how we are dealing with "the grammar issue" in our classrooms, teacher-training programs, and interactions with the public.

In addition to "issues of grammar," there are other aspects of revising and editing, sometimes presented as "rules," which are really more like myths or folk beliefs. One concerns "topic sentences." Over a quarter-century ago, Richard Braddock's study of twenty-five essays picked at random from respected journals such as *Harpers* and *The New Yorker* suggested that the conventional textbook claims regarding the existence and placement of "topic" sentences in an essay could not be substantiated (296–301). It's not that Braddock's study is the last word on topic sentences. It's not that topic sentences don't exist or are not useful in ways the grammar books claim. But sometimes academic or public laments about students' perceived ignorance regarding topic sentences proceed as if Braddock never complicated the issue. Mostly there isn't even a discussion, only an assumption that published writing has such things as topic sentences and that student writing should have more of them.

One way to address both legitimate concerns and myths about topic sentences is to use Richard Beach's suggestion that writers identify (either out loud to a peer or by writing in the margins) what each paragraph or section of a draft is doing: what it *shows* rather than what it *says* (in Anson 1989, 133). This by itself might suggest revising ideas because it forces writers to look not at individual sentences, but to step back and look at the piece holistically and then by section and paragraph. It helps them relate parts to whole. The Tinkertoy work described in Chapter 3 might accomplish the same thing with appropriate prompts. Writers might do these or similar exercises after having just read or heard about Braddock's research on topic sentences.

Students should also be made aware of controversies in Composition about stylistic advice. Over twenty years ago, Richard Ohmann questioned widely accepted grammar handbook advice to "use definite, specific, concrete language" (390). Pointing to an "ideology of style" that admonishes students to fill their essays with concrete details, Ohmann argues that we may be stifling a more meaningful, metaphorical style. His decades-old statement about power is still relevant: "in the cause of improving their skills, we may end up increasing their powerlessness" (396–97).

Students should also know about Stephen P. Witte's and Lester Faigley's studies of high-rated and low-rated essays—and their implications. In general Witte and Faigley found "that high-rated essays are longer and contain larger T-units and clauses, more nonrestrictive modifiers, and fewer errors" (195). What is interesting is their summary and then complication of M. A. K. Halliday's and Ruqauya Hansan's work with textual cohesion, which they separate into two types: endophoric, the semantic ties within a text that relate one part to another; and exophoric, the elements that lie outside a text (189–90). Witte's and Faigley's work showed that high-rated essays had more "collocations," or elaborations and examples than the lower-rated ones (198). But in the end they are careful not to recommend the direct teaching of elaboration because so many issues related to "cohesion" are related to factors outside the text, including what factors relevant to the *reader* affect the "cohesion" of the text (199–202). In other words, textual features alone cannot determine whether a text is coherent or cohesive. Its clarity depends also on who is reading it, when, where, and why.

Harping on "grammar" gives the message that "writing" *is* grammar, which can be and often is easily binarized into a what-is-right discussion, the above complications notwithstanding—and usually not discussed. How can we deal with revising and editing so that students both understand the importance of well-edited prose as well as the complex, inexact, socially constructed process that results in what gets defined as "well-edited" prose? How can we help writers (and readers) see that "standard" English is, as Keith Gilyard points out, "standard-ized" English?[3]

Using Multiple Channels

In spite of all the caveats we must juggle as we help students revise and edit their work, there are some multiple-channel strategies that can help students rethink an argument, revisit a claim, or reconceptualize an entire project. Here is one that uses the physical re-positioning of paragraphs as a tool for rethinking the whole text, as well as for revising parts of it.

As do the index-cards-manipulation exercise described in Chapter 3, cutting and pasting paragraphs challenges students to reconceptualize organizational patterns in an essay or paper. It also helps them see results of paragraphing decisions and choices regarding transitional sentences or words. For this exercise, I am indebted to Anna McMullen, an instructor at Utica College of Syracuse University, whose class I observed actively engaged in this activity.

Cutting and Pasting Paragraphs

First, students come to class with typed copies of their drafts, as well as scissors and tape. Writers remove any staples from their drafts, as well as top margins, page numbers, or anything else that might indicate original paragraph order. They then cut the paper apart by paragraph, and shuffle the order, and leave them in a neat pile on their desks. Then they switch seats with a neighbor. Now each student must put someone else's paragraphs in some kind of logical order, based on content and possible argumentative purpose, taping their selections together. When that's completed, students change seats again, with the new reader looking at the now taped-together essay. This new reader may agree with and initial the taped version, or decide on yet another paragraph order, indicating the new order by numbering his or her choice.

Then writers return to their original seats and see what others have done to the order of their paragraphs. After students have a chance to study the results, they can write about it, draw, or discuss with the class what it might mean if the new paragraph orders are identical or similar to, or radically different from, their original. Any result, of course, could indicate desirable or undesirable features of the writer's original text, but the benefits of the task for both writers and re-organizers comes in the active analysis of real text, in physically manipulating paragraphs and seeing the resulting change in emphasis.

Not only does this kinesthetic work with ideas help all learners experiment with organizational patterns, it also clearly exemplifies the role of transitions and the effects of unusually long or short paragraphs and/or sentences. Writers returning to their own work can see how someone else reconceived their argument, and writers also return better able to view their own work through a reader's lens, better able to predict a reader's misunderstandings.

This exercise is multisensory in a way that word-processed cutting and pasting is not. Moving paragraphs around on a computer screen has been with us for decades. However, moving the paper paragraphs around like puzzle pieces demonstrates each change even as it allows writers to get a sense of how the entire essay changes when one paragraph is moved. It also has students getting up and moving to different desks. Writers obtain both metacognitive and physical distance on their work, and then return to it with a number of different perspectives.

Sketching and Crossing out Sections of Typical Drafts

Crossing out sections of typical drafts is another way to help writers better conceive of their entire draft as a piece of clay they can manipulate as a whole (rather than just in atoms of word choice and spelling). The following demonstration stemmed from frustrating (and failed) attempts to get students to do more than run a spell checker when revising early drafts. From years of directing a writing center and reading many early drafts, I knew that for some writers, an early "draft" was really no more than what resulted from a fifteen-minute directed freewrite. Nevertheless, it might be several pages long, and busy students were loathe to add to or change their texts in any substantive way. Deleting or starting over was out of the question.

Freewrites often have kernels of intriguing ideas, as Elbow has shown, but more often than not, the writer arrives at those ideas near the end of the writing session that produced the "draft." More often than not, the last paragraph or so of a three-page draft revealed insights arrived at *after* the writer had produced a few pages of thinking on paper, focusing on the topic, playing with ideas. Sometimes, if writers begin the next draft with the last paragraph of their first draft, it pushes them in a direction in which the first draft helped them discover they wanted to go. However, if they cling to the first few pages, which may represent a meandering series of false starts ("throat-clearing," someone has called it), their "revised draft" may be nothing more than well-edited chaos. The first pages may have served their purpose in the early draft of helping the writer focus, but once the writer has discovered that focus, the early meandering can be removed like training wheels from a bicycle. It slows down the rider/writer to keep support that's no longer needed.

To illustrate this concept, I sketch on the board or overhead what this kind of early draft looks like (see Figure 4–1). I use lines to represent text. Then I circle the last paragraph or so, advising writers to examine it closely for the "center of gravity" Elbow says first drafts can reveal. I also dramatically cross out the first two pages, explaining that deleting large sections of text might be the most helpful approach to beginning a new draft. A graduate school professor (Gene Mirabelli, at SUNY Albany) once said in a creative writing workshop that one way to emphasize a point was to eliminate the distracters. This invaluable ad-

Figure 4–1
Circling and crossing out sections of typical drafts

vice, given to fiction writers, applies to academic writers as well. The first draft reveals things. Then it should be sifted for its plumpest kernels and the rest discarded.

Something about sketching these hypothetical drafts on the board and then crossing out huge sections of them dramatizes for students the value of deep, radical revision in a much more powerful way than simply telling them to make more than surface-level changes. Not every last paragraph is a gem, of course, and not every early portion of a first draft should be thrown out. I draw alternate versions of hypothetical drafts on the board, circling different sections and crossing out different paragraphs. The point is to show how a first draft can be revised, not sentence by sentence or word by word, but totally reconceived in subsequent drafts that are more focused and more powerful not only for what's been added, but also what's been deleted. This sketched demonstration can be done graphically, as shown in Figure 4–1, on a black or white board, a flip chart, or an overhead. A three-dimensional version of it might use Legos, Tinkertoys, modeling clay, multi-colored pipe cleaners, or people.

The Hunt for "Padding"

Another way to get writers thinking about major revisions, especially deletions, is to ask them to locate "padding"—chunks of text variously called "tangents," "Engfish" (Ken Macrorie's term for the overinflated chunks common in the writing of English majors), or by a less euphemisic, barnyard-related metaphor. Padding can be unnecessarily repeated ideas, unrelated experience, inflated language, irrelevant information, or any sentence or paragraph that detracts from, rather than adds to, what seems to be a writer's overall purpose. Padding is common in school writing because it can stretch a paper that might not fit minimum word or page length requirements. Experienced and inexperienced writers are equally familiar with this material. They've all written it, and they all know it when they see it. Teachers read it because they have to. It bores everyone.

Writers may resist parting with sections of their own texts, but they are less hesitant to assist in chopping out padded sections of classmates' drafts. Here are questions that can direct peer responders to help writers locate unneeded sentences or paragraphs:

- Can you point to any sections of this draft that might have been added as padding to stretch the paper.
- What sections are unnecessary, repetitive, or irrelevant?
- What could be crossed out without harming the overall draft?
- What sections, if gone, might even help clarify the overall purpose of the draft?

Once students understand what it is they're looking for, they can easily spot it. In fact, whenever I ask students to help their classmates seek out and destroy padding, there are many knowing nods and grins.

Once they've irradicated it in a classmate's paper, they return to their own drafts more open to finding and eliminating it in their own.

Thinking in these ways is analogous to viewing a painting or listening to music from different perspectives: studying the foreground and then the background, and then both together. How do the details contribute to the overall effect? How does the overall effect change when the viewer shifts position in relation to the painting, or the listener plays with treble and bass adjustments? Students might look at early sketches of paintings or different cuts of famous songs to see how artists change and revise their work.

Padding with a Purpose

Another way to help students think about reorganizing their essays in substantial ways is to follow the "padding" hunt described above with a discussion that contradicts it. In other words, sometimes "padding" has a purpose. Sometimes text that appears in relation to the bulk of the draft to be "padding" may actually reveal the direction in which the writer really wants to go. Drawing on Jane Gallup's interpretation of a photography-related term and metaphor used by Roland Barthes, Julie Jung explains that in photography, the "stadium" is the main idea within the picture, but that it is the more interesting "punctum," the "unexpected detail" or "disruption" that invites an audience to look beyond the frame, that "offer[s] proof that revision is possible." Jung argues that we should "highlight the disruption rather than gloss over it, or worse yet, explain it away" (438–39). Similarly, the hunt for padding, informed by a discussion of "punctum," can help writers consider exploring further the intriguing slips, the rich code, they might have previously deleted as tangents.

Writers and readers alike need to be alert for these hints or traces of meaning, which is impossible if they've got their noses to the paper combing for comma and spelling errors. They'll miss the potentially big picture and re-organizing potential that an apparently "irrelevant" paragraph or sentence can provide. Readers can learn how to be attuned to these revelatory tangents in early drafts: the road not taken, but should have been. The point is to get people thinking differently about their own "tangents" and how they might not be extraneous after all, but road signs or pointers. Unless *readers* approach drafts globally, however, the text will not yield these invaluable clues. Copy editors do not discover them. People who have had the "five-paragraph theme" too entrenched in their minds as a template for reading or writing drafts—and this can be English teachers as well as the conventionally "good writers" in the class—are sometimes the people least able to help writers re-interpret drafts, with their sometimes purposeful tangents, as blueprints for major re-organization. People who typically do well with school writing can greatly benefit sometimes from people not as steeped in conventional organizational patterns. Students with social, kinesthetic, or mathematical talents might be more likely to recognize "departures" from the theme as arrows to the writer's subliminal purpose, even when the writer herself might not recognize them.

Getting writers to reconceptualize and reorganize drafts, as writing teachers well know, is a Herculean task. Radical reorganization is also sometimes the only chance a draft has of being substantially improved. *Telling* students to make global changes is useless. *Showing* them how to do so by using unconventional and multisensory strategies is a more dramatic and productive use of time. Designing peer response strategies that take advantage of the insights and perspectives of all learners, not just those with linguistic talents, challenges everyone to make radical, global revisions.

Listening to Drafts

Listening to a draft (rather than reading it with red pen in hand) is much more conducive to hearing these departures from a "main" idea, both tangential departures as well as the important revelatory kind. Many Composition scholars have long promoted the efficacy of reading aloud in detecting overall purpose and tone (see Moffett, Ponsot and Deen, Berthoff, and others). Knoblauch and Brannon (1984) have also argued that the drafting process should attend to "first things first," which means that although the writing process is not linear, it makes sense to engage writers in the kind of "dialectical *process*" that will engage their imagination and help them discover their meaning (Berthoff's emphasis, 1981, 39–40). While holistic composing and reading strategies are not new to Composition classes, the silent reading of written drafts by "peer editors" too often ignores the multisensory advantages of oral reading and concentrated listening. When students listen to each other's drafts, several things happen. The listeners hone their listening concentration and practice analyzing both the overall purpose and structure of the text and then articulating their reactions to it. The writers get to hear their work out loud, which by itself can tell them which sentences sound choppy, which ones are never-ending, which ones are confusing, causing readers to trip. They also get perspectives from students who might be alert close editors, as well as from students who might be overall analysts, able to provide insightful, forest-like overviews not possible if readers are inspecting trees or examining leaves.

Effective writing center pedagogy has long taken advantage of the fact that if inexperienced tutors silently read a written draft, they almost invariably begin to address editorial issues of correctness before a writer has had a chance to let overall meaning fully crystallize. In contrast, hearing a piece read out loud by the writer helps tutors or peer readers listen for important issues such as overall purpose, voice, organization, thesis, evidence, examples, and so on. If one of those global issues is inchoate or even completely out of whack, the writer needs to find out now, when global changes are more palatable, not after he or she has carefully edited for run-ons, verb-tense agreement, spelling, and the like. Many writing center directors wisely train peer tutors to have writers read their work out loud, allowing the tutor to do some alert listening. In fact, if writers seem particularly frustrated, sometimes it's best to put the draft aside for a while. The reader/tutor can interview the writer, with an open-ended question such as, "What is the purpose of this project?" This should get the writer talking, and therefore thinking. Having sketch pads, Legos, sticky notes, or other materials available might be helpful to students at this point. This technique of *listening* to ideas or drafts, a common and successful approach in writing centers, works well as a classroom strategy also. It can be used for generating or organizing ideas, as discussed in Chapter 3, or later for paragraph- or sentence-level responses.

Metaphors

Metaphors work like multisensory strategies because, as discussed in Chapter 3, they force unlike things together, shifting perspective or blending images (the child's laugh was a wind chime). I discovered their power several years ago when I was teaching a Women in World Literature course to upper-level English majors. I was frustrated with their first drafts of analytical papers because all they were doing was summarizing what this or that critic had said about the writer or text they were studying. These were people I knew had insightful, somewhat original things to say, yet they clung to dead critics like life preservers, fronting decades-old ideas instead of their own. The students' analyses became a weak "me-too" listing of critics' views, instead of the critics' views providing a quick, legitimizing ethos to the students as members of a discourse community with authority to speak about these texts. I had tried *telling* them to foreground their own ideas and to soft-pedal the critics. "Use more of your own ideas," I said. That did nothing.

I needed to help writers see their drafts in a different way, to disrupt their business-as-usual approach to churning out a paper and revising a draft by tending to cosmetic niceties. My driver education experience kicked in again as I suddenly came up with this metaphor: "You do the driving for this paper," I said, and I drew a car on the board. "You are in the driver's seat. You plan the route. Put the critics in the

back seat. Don't even let them look at the map." In fact, I said, "You may
want to put them in the trunk." (Now I had their attention.) "If you get
hopelessly lost," I continued, "you may want to stop the car, open the
trunk, and allow them to say a word or two, but this is your trip." At
this point, they were all laughing, and they knew what I was talking
about. I had been putting my list of dos and don'ts on the board, and at
this point, someone asked, "Can we add to the list?" Class members
added the second half of this extended metaphor:

> You are in the driver's seat of this critical paper.
>
> You do the driving.
>
> You plan the route.
>
> You hold the map.
>
> Put the critics in the back seat.
>
> Don't even let them look at the map.
>
> Put them in the trunk if they won't keep quiet.
>
> Pop the trunk and ask their opinion only when you need it.
>
> Don't drive around the same block twice.
>
> Signal all turns.
>
> Be careful of detours.
>
> Don't run out of gas before the end of the trip.

One student from that class e-mailed me long after she graduated. She
said she had a vivid memory of that day we did the driver's seat
metaphor in class and that it had helped her through many subsequent
writing projects.

I've also used metaphors with students to help them conceptualize
why proofreading tasks are important. I tell them that a brand-new
house might be designed very well, have a solid foundation and plenty
of closet space and insulation. But these might not be immediately obvious to a buyer who enters the house for a final walk-through before
the closing. If there are cigarette butts in the kitchen sink, fast-food
wrappers on the counter, or wallpaper scraps on the floor, the potential owner might be distracted from noticing the cathedral ceilings or
stylish chandeliers. So by itself, I say, one empty paint can left in the
garage is not important. But three or four can make a buyer reconsider
the entire sale, thinking perhaps that the sloppy things she *can* see are
indicative of the state of things she can't see, such as beams, pipes, insulation, and electrical wires. So before you open the house to potential buyers, I say, pull up the drop cloths, throw away the cigarette butts,
wash the windows, and shine the faucets and sinks. A vacuumed car-

pet doesn't make a house more solid, but one covered with sawdust and paint chips can draw attention away from things you want someone to really appreciate.

A Word About Assessment

Before, during, or after students respond to each others' drafts regarding matters of editing and revising, they should discuss and/or help determine or negotiate how their writing will be judged in the context of the particular assignment. How much does surface correctness "count"? What about level of risk taken by the writer? What about the project's relevance to world issues? Is responding to others' drafts part of the evaluation? Many Composition teacher/scholars have addressed issues of assessment (Peter Elbow, Brian Huot, Kathleen Blake Yancey, Bob Broad, etc.). Peter Elbow has suggested putting as many evaluative factors as are consciously available on the table for discussion and clarity (1993). Lee Odell has students look at high-, middle-, and lowrated past essays of the type they are now being asked to produce.[4] My purpose here is not to summarize every major theory regarding assessment. The point is, students should be privy to research and disagreements regarding assessment and what it suggests about the way some writing has been judged. Even for undergraduates, a brief foray into well-known Composition research about grading might help them develop a more conscious awareness of what factors in the past have impacted different judges' perception of text quality. Complicating notions of how writing gets evaluated provides a different perspective to students who may believe there is such a thing as an ideal text, as well as an ideal way to respond to one.

To help students become more conscious of what they value as readers, and why, students might read or be told about the research Paul Diederich and his colleagues did in 1961, as described in his 1974 text, *Measuring Growth in English*. This elegant piece of older research should help students abandon myths of ideal texts or ideal judgments about them, which in turn can help them take more seriously their writing and their peer responding.

Without the customary norming sessions the Educational Testing Service oversees before a "real" evaluation of student writing, this experiment had 53 people from a variety of disciplines and careers rank 300 student papers. They were instructed to read them at home and to put them in 9 piles "in order of general merit." There were to be at least 12 papers in each of the piles (5). The results were riotously scattered: "out of the 300 essays graded, 101 received every grade from 1 to

9; 94 percent received either seven, eight, or nine different grades; and no essay received less than five different grades from these fifty-three readers" (6).

After analyzing the written comments of the judges, the researchers found some patterns. First, "the largest cluster" of readers ranked the papers primarily for their "ideas expressed: their richness, soundness, clarity, development, and relevance to the topic and the writer's purpose" (6). As responders to their peers' writing, students need to know this lest they set about concentrating solely on copy editing issues in the draft. Next in matter of importance to the judges, especially to those who were college English instructors, was what I have been calling surface correctness: "errors in usage, sentence structure, punctuation, and spelling" (7). The third-highest factor was something the researchers called "organization and analysis" (7–8), though it seems to me that those categories might overlap with the "development" and "richness" aspects included in the first category. The fourth aspect valued by readers was related to wording, phrasing, and vocabulary (8). The fifth-highest comments, and ones which came primarily from those readers Diederich characterized as creative writers, "emphasized style, individuality, originality, interest, and sincerity—the *personal qualities* revealed by the writing, which we decided to call 'flavor,' although they themselves called it 'style'" (8).

After conducting this analysis, the researchers concluded that even these five factors they were able to discern among the different readers accounted for only part of the difference in grading. They pointed out that the same readers might grade differently if given the papers at a different time and place (10). If this experiment doesn't confuse things enough, there is Benjamin Rosner's work, cited by Diederich, in which one set of essays stamped "honors" was evaluated by one group of teachers; the same set was stamped "regular" and graded by another set. Contrary to the researchers' expectations, "the papers that were stamped 'honors' averaged almost one grade-point higher than the other copies of the very same papers that were stamped 'regular'" (12). Commenting on why this happened, Diederich says, "we find what we expect to find" (12).

Diederich's fifth factor regarding "good" writing's display of "sincerity" and "individuality" supports William E. Coles, Jr.,'s and James Vopat's research, cited by Lester Faigley in *Fragments of Rationality* (120–26). A majority of the forty-eight writing teachers, researchers, and theorists Coles and Vopat asked to participate in their research on assessment consistently valued "personal experience" essays that they described as "authentic," "honest," or "truthful." Faigley sees this as evidence that Composition is overly focused on the concept of an individual self, as opposed to being more critically aware of what he sees as a more sophisticated, post-modern view of the multiplicity of constructed selves. However, the Coles/Vopat research Faigley cites here is useful because it puts on the table what specific influential English professors value in a text. This knowledge can help students step away from the table, get an overview of these values, and then judge the judgments. They can then make more informed decisions about what they will include or delete from their own texts, and why.

These older but fascinating experiments would open discussions about the relationships between and among readers, writers, and texts. As Diederich points out, "few if any readers are conscious of what they are actually responding to in student writing that makes them grade one paper higher than another" (8–9). Discussing these or similar experiments, or participating in informal ones like these, might help peer and teacher responders become more conscious of the textual features that affect them, as well as the socially constructed reasons why. Having even a passing familiarity with research that shows the inexact science involved in "grading a paper" may help students become more alert responders, as well as more sophisticated contributors to future school board and community debates about "standards" and "writing quality."

There are an almost infinite supply of studies and practices that could muddy the waters around notions of "good" and "bad" writing, which in turn complicate strategies, multisensory or otherwise, used to teach writing. These complications range from the deeply held prejudices about people such as the kind Victor Villanueva describes, to the perhaps unconscious valuing of the perceived "authenticity" or "originality" of a text commented on by Lester Faigley, to the simpler, but just as culturally complicated notions of the infamous "comma splice"—i.e., what it is and isn't and who can and cannot use it. As Knoblauch and Brannon point out, "Competent writers regularly violate technical rules, the comma splice included, while unpracticed writers often manage to avoid technical lapses without thereby much enhancing the quality of their texts" (1984, 153). Lester Faigley notes that comma splices can be found across a spectrum of respected publications today, and that this practice "may reflect a relaxing of formal conventions that has been underway throughout this [20th] century" (203 in *Fragments of Rationality*). Sharon Crowley and Debra Hawhee acknowledge most composition graders' rabid hatred of sentence fragments. However, they call the conventional "fragment" definition "nonsense [that] derives from an eighteenth-century superstition about sentences, which supposed that every sentence represents a complete thought. Whatever that is" (284).

Why then, do people in authority pay so much attention to "fragments," "comma splices," and other linguistic sins that some writers are allowed to commit and others are not? One reason of course is Sharon Crowley's point that these things provide a handy tool for discrimination when needed. A less sinister, but still not admirable, reason is posited by Donald Daiker, who argues that it is much easier for reader-judges to tell writers what they are doing "wrong" than it is to take the time to analyze and articulate their strengths (1989, 110–11).

Issues of revising and editing are important not because they concern "correctness," but because they concern socially constructed *perceptions* of correctness which we and our students ignore at our peril. These commonplaces about "correct" English are infused with so many elements that it's tempting not to deal with editing at all. On the other hand, it's possible to focus entirely on revising and editing. That's because discussing notions of "correctness" by following all the complex paths Crowley, Villanueva, Williams, Diederich, and others have shown us, can raise issues related to every other aspect of "writing": audience, purpose, context, voice, evaluation, assignment, neatness, etc. Even the dismissal or taken-for-grantedness of "well-edited prose" could be the subject of an upper-level graduate course on the theoretical assumptions informing that phrase.

Sharon Crowley points out that the curriculum for Freshman English is thought of as "cultural capital—as the mutual property of all persons who conceive of education as a site for transmission of received dominant culture" (1998, 231). No wonder, she says, that it engenders such heated debates. She goes on to explain how "correctness" functions as a gatekeeper:

> In America's cultural imagination, mastery of "correct" English still signifies that its users are suitable for admission to the class of educated persons. This is generally wielded negatively; that is, "correct" English is used as a handy standard of exclusion by those who practice racial or class discrimination. (231)

Confusion as Conduit

What all this means is that we may leave students confused about issues of revising, editing, "grammar," and "correctness." This is a good thing. Confusion is a conduit for productive sparks, the friction needed to keep us and our students rethinking writing and its reception in our society. As Paulo Freire understood, certainty about theory and practice stifles praxis because praxis involves a continuous dialectic about what and how to teach. In *Rhetorical Traditions*, Knoblauch and Brannon rightly warn against an uninformed mixing of teaching theories that contradict each other and epistemological assumptions that may confuse students.

However, as the foregoing discussion of revising and editing issues has shown, there are contradictions students need to negotiate for themselves. People *are* judged by their language use, *and* they are also judged by other things that sometimes parade as issues of language. A reader's perception of a writer's "errors" can deeply affect that writer's ethos, yet what a reader perceives as error varies with the perceived authority of both writer and reader. Writers and peer readers need to pay attention to the ideas in a draft, but they also have to pay homage to situational constraints as they go from one rhetorical situation to the next.

What this might mean in practice is that we need to talk about specific ways to remember the details of perceived correctness, even as we talk about why those perceptions can vary so much. One example is a conversation I used to have more in the 1980s than I do today. It concerned the use of gendered pronoun use. At writing center staff meetings, we talked about ways to both answer writers' questions about whether to use "he," "she," "they," or "he/she," and also to understand the possible effect that choice can have on intended readers. In other words, students need to know the ever-changing rules of a variety of games, even as they learn to question the game.

To return to the closet/clothing metaphor: After we have examined all the items and thrown some away, there may be things we cannot use, but cannot yet discard. Even the cheap fads of long ago may be rediscovered by a new generation (i.e., the return of polyester, kerchiefs, pant suits, and bell bottoms).

Copying sentences is one example of an oddity that might "work" in ways we don't yet understand. In their rhetoric textbook, Crowley and Hawhee remind us that ancient rhetoricians often had their students read aloud to develop both reading skills as well as a way to listen for rhythm and style. Or they would have their students copy favorite passages word-for-word into a commonplace book, the act of copying aiding memory and copiousness, and the slow motion of the hand copying helping writers "focus on the passage being copied" (293–94).

As old as this practice is, it is consistent with Arthur S. Reber's 1967 research, cited by Patrick Hartwell, that "demonstrated that mere exposure to grammatical sentences produced tacit learning: subjects who copied several grammatical sentences performed far above chance in judging the grammaticality of other letter strings" (1985, 117; Reber research is footnote 17). These results are also consistent with writers' stories of themselves as avid readers since early childhood. Those who read a lot may internalize grammatical structures in ways that cannot "be taught" directly. Yet not everyone loves to read, and they are our students, too—smart in ways we who think in words may not be capable of fully understanding.

I think we are stuck with this contradiction: that we must help students negotiate the shoals of "correctness" even as we try to expose how those sandbars can shift with time and tide, and how some people get to sail over them in yachts while others run aground in heavy fishing vessels. That we may have to use a combination of approaches—even opposite, epistemologically conflicting approaches—to help students negotiate this danger, does not spring from an easy eclecticism. Rather, it comes from strategic, difficult maneuvering in fairly dirty water, not unlike the task of effective rhetors.

We can use the revising/editing/grammar/correctness debate as a point of departure for the more complete debate that needs to take place in our classrooms, in our department meetings, in our College Councils, and in our local and national newspapers. We may be weary of the fight. But if we who have the most background in the complexities of this issue refuse to engage those who don't, we have only ourselves to blame for the prevalence of simplistic declarations about "correctness," "grammar," and "proper English" that we may have had shoved in the "case closed" file in the back of the closet for decades. As Fox points out, we need to hold "intelligent and respectful conversations about composition with people who are uninformed" (113). How to do this effectively is the subject of Chapter 6.

Editing and revising is a drama about power. It has simple or elaborate costumes, depending on the play, and its success depends on its debut city and sophistication level of its audience. Instead of simply being given a list of which lights to dim or which curtains to draw, students should take a backstage tour of the whole production, as well as a peek at the financial backers. Since the entire production involves reading as well as writing, the next chapter suggests ways to use multiple literacies to analyze texts.

Notes

1. *Ancient Rhetorics for Contemporary Students,* p. 283.

2. For an examination of the grammar controversy from a Vygotskian perspective, see Chapter 14 of James Thomas Zebroski's *Thinking Through Theory.*

3. "Identities and the 'Dream': Dilemmas for Composition at the Turn of the Century" (Chair's Address), CCCC 2000, April 13, 2000, Minneapolis.

4. In the late 1980s, at Maria College in Albany, New York, I attended a very useful workshop Lee Odell led on this strategy.

Chapter Five

Using Non-Writing
to Analyze Reading

Many of the alternate strategies discussed so far regarding the teaching of writing can be modified for use in classes where students are analyzing or critiquing texts, often a crucial part of a writing task. This might include courses in textual studies, linguistics, English education, children's literature, rhetoric or composition theory, literary or cultural criticism, or courses across the curriculum. Instructors should consider how visualization, physical activity, or other non-writing work might demonstrate, at least analogously, a concept relevant to course readings. Such approaches do not take the place of reading, but they can supplement whatever intellectual processes people use to explore, compare, analyze, or problematize texts. This chapter discusses select activities meant to spark the imagination of instructors committed to using multiple ways of knowing in a variety of classes. Before using these or related activities, of course, instructors should make them consistent to their own course goals and philosophical beliefs about learning. What is it that students should "know" or be able to do at the end of this assignment, class, course, or program? What intellectual processes should a reading, discussion, writing or other project help students develop?[1]

North's "Fusion" Model and His
Students' "Recombinatory" Projects

In his recent book, *Refiguring the Ph.D. in English Studies,* Stephen M. North (with Barbara A. Chepaitis, David Coogan, Lâle Davidson, Ron MacLean, Cindy L. Parrish, Jonathan Post, and Beth Weatherby) describes a number of performance-based projects his graduate students did in response to theoretical readings. His description of their work provides a good starting place for the suggestions in this chapter. First, some context: North proposes that English departments use the friction of their conflicts productively to create a "fusion-based" curriculum, one that would bring the "disparate elements together under sufficient pressure and with sufficient energy to transform them into a single new entity, one quite distinct from any of the original components" (73).[2]

In his description of a course he has taught representative of those offered in the fusion model, North lists a number of different genres graduate students in his History of English Studies have used in addition to traditional essays: "short stories, text-only and text-and-image collages, poems, taped audio performances (in the manner of a radio broadcast), plays and scripted skits, StorySpace constructions and Web sites, first-person narratives, puzzles, videos and multimedia productions, and so on" (132). He follows this list with three extended examples of how these projects were a melding of "topic, form and method" (132).

Even less traditional projects were produced by graduate students doing what North calls "recombinatory" writing, that is, a mixing of genres analogous to the "nexus of discourses" represented in SUNY Albany's English department. He describes the resulting mergers as "the microresults of the program's macroprocesses, (by)products of its ongoing fusion experiment. As such, they are often both unfamiliar and relatively unstable: strange, evanescent, short-lived creatures" (165). Two of the many examples he gives: One pair of students, in response to Jasper Neel's book, *Plato, Derrida, and Writing,* constructed a "conversation" using selected passages from both Plato and Derrida. Another student wrote a parody, with Frederick Jameson as an operator of a dude ranch. (North's descriptions of both of these need to be read for full effect.) He gives a longer account of one student's final project in Composition Theory, which is a recombinatory piece that includes narration, dreamscape, multiple beginnings, reflections on the multiple beginnings, and a Venn diagram. North emphasizes that what distinguishes this project and others described in this section of his book is "the *relationship* it established among its discursively differentiated parts: the way it brought together, and in particular coordinated, topics, forms, and methods traditionally associated with rhetoric and composition, creative writing, and personal autobiography" (his emphasis, 179–84).

In a section both acknowledging and critiquing "the primacy of print" in English Studies, North recommends performance as a relatively uncharted opportunity in which to explore ideas, discourses, and alternative formats. He points out the irony that in spite of English instructors' need to use performance-related skills such as speaking and moving in their teaching, department meetings, conferences, etc., these skills have not been considered important, and students have not been taught these skills directly. Instead, students must depend on an "unarticulated pattern of socialization" (189). Because performance is still relatively uncharted territory in English Studies, North argues, it might be "a useful medium for fusion experiments, a largely unpoliced arena in which to (re)combine elements from across intradisciplinary lines" (189–90).

He gives a partial list of what some Albany graduate students have done with performance-related projects in The History of English Studies course: "marionette and puppet shows, room-sized floor puzzles, poems performed in multiple voices, multimedia presentations (e.g., video- and audiotape supplemented with PowerPoint), in-class presentations for voice and saxophone, installations—you get the idea" (190).

The point is we can use the power generated by epistemological and other differences in most English departments as a generative rather than destructive force: "the object would be to harness the energy generated by the conflicts in order to forge some new disciplinary enterprise altogether" (73). The most electrifying moments of fusion would occur in class projects (not "papers") as graduate students of many persuasions (rhetoricians, compositionists, linguists, creative writers, cultural critics, educators, literary theorists, etc.) would grapple together with readings and reactions, forging "recombinatory" projects in which form and content blur and spark. The potential and the problem of such intellectual work would force all involved to rethink and revisit conventional assumptions about writing, reading, interpreting text, as well as the overall purpose of English Studies.

Multiple Intelligences in the Secondary Schools

On the secondary school level, there are a number of people who have suggested multi-model strategies, especially in literature classes. College professors have much to learn from them about working with different modalities. Even if students are to do something as simple as summarize a writer's argument, they might supplement a conventional written summary by taking advantage of "multiple channels" to help them conceptualize ideas, concepts, or opinions in the readings. Alternate strategies can also help students analyze text on multiple levels of understanding, analysis, and critique.

Peter Smagorinsky, in *Expressions*, discusses many options for using multiple intelligences in interpreting literary texts: provide musical background to an oral reading of the text; put on a puppet show; do a parody, a sculpture, a collage, a dance, a map, or a mix of photos, video, or hypermedia in a presentation about a text. In their book *Inside Out: Developmental Strategies for Teaching Writing,* Dan Kirby, Tom Liner, and Ruth Vinz suggest similar approaches: having students design a book jacket for the novel under discussion, or create a map illustrating the character's main actions (176).

In 1995, there was an entire issue of *English Journal* (the NCTE publication for secondary-level) devoted to multiple intelligences (M-I). In most articles, the stated or assumed purpose of most of the strategies is to help students "interpret literature," with little or no questioning of which texts are considered "literature," what kinds of interpretations are used, or why. Nevertheless, the strategies can be adapted in a variety of text-centered college courses and used to help students engage the readings from a number of perspectives. Smagorinsky, also writing in the M-I issue of *English Journal,* has his students do "transmediations" (he cites Suhor's use of the term), or interpretations of one genre using another. For example, in response to Williams' story "The Use of Force," Smagorinsky's students might draw a picture, choreograph a dance, create a soundtrack, or write a drama (22).

These suggestions are similar to my use of "companion pieces" and "parallel stories" as a way to respond to a text. When I taught a women's literature course several years ago, I offered as an option to a conventional paper that students could write a companion piece or parallel story to the play or piece of fiction we discussed in class. These pieces could take several forms: a prequel or sequel to a story; a story or dramatic scene from a different character's point of view; a contemporary retelling of an older piece; or a parallel story using a format similar to the one we read for class. For example, they could write an original story using the daydream/reality pattern from "The Secret Life of Walter Mitty," or from Ambrose Bierce's "An Occurrence at Owl Creek Bridge." One young woman wrote a re-telling of Zora Neale Hurston's "The Gilded Six Bits," a story in which the writer experiments with omniscient and objective point of view to achieve a certain effect. This student retold the story in first person, from Missie May's point of view, completely changing what gets emphasized, which in turn makes Hurston's choices even more meaningful. These companion pieces sometimes stand alone as implied commentary on the original text, or they can be contextualized explicitly within a theoretical framework. Original dramatizations of fictional work can be discussed in class or used to launch further analyses.

In another article in the M-I issue of *English Journal,* Richard Gage has over fifty options his students can choose from for their literature projects. They might design library displays, mobiles, plot diagrams, time lines, character portraits, or CD jackets. They might do small-group role-plays of epilogues to texts such as *The Glass Menagerie,* where students act out possible future plans for the main characters. Gage cites Judith C. Reiff as suggesting that hyperactivity diagnoses in children may be a failure to recognize and use kinesthetic talents. Citing Walter Barbe and Michael Milone, Gage points out that people who learn kinesthetically comprise about 15 percent of the population (53).

Bruce Pirie, who also had a piece in that special issue, has his students interpret William Golding's *Lord of the Flies* by having them design "choral readings" that foreground important exchanges in the novel between the characters. Here is his description:

> groups of students copy down lines said by Jack or Ralph (one character assigned per group)—lines that highlight the tension emerging between the two boys. When they string these quotations together, the groups have, in effect, created monologues to be delivered chorally, with movements, face-to-face against an "opposing" group—a "Jack" group and a "Ralph" group presenting their monologues to each other in sequence. ("Jack" groups often invade the space of the "Ralph" group, encircling or penetrating the other group, a kinesthetic embodiment of Jack's aggressive drive.)(47)

He then combines this kinesthetic, oral, and visual activity by having students discuss and write about it afterward. As Pirie points out, kinesthetic approaches do not isolate only one talent: "Typically, students move (kinesthetically), see others move (visually), talk about it (verbally and interpersonally), and reflect on it (intrapersonally)" (50). Pirie employs a number of other conceptualizations. Students, in silence, walk in slow motion the way a literary character might, or become "statues" representing a character, or dramatize "dreamscapes" inspired by characters dreamt adventures in *The Divine Comedy, Alice in Wonderland,* and *A Christmas Carol* (47–48).[3]

Pirie warns about dangers that students may view "fun" activities as a frivolous escape from what is perceived as a more serious "meaning-making mode." To counter this, he tells students that after the activity is over, they will have to discuss it or write about it (49). It is sad that he must to begin this way, but given received judgments in society about enjoyment, drudgery, and learning, as John Mayher has shown, it might be necessary. Colleagues' views may also be entrenched against taking these approaches seriously. Pirie recounts, "When I offered teachers a workshop called Learning English Through the Body, a friendly skeptic asked, 'Is that as opposed to through the brain?'" As Pirie points out, that question is a false opposition. Similarly, Peter Smagorinsky says that some of his more skeptical colleagues commented that students were just "playing games" (20).

There are other suggestions from that M-I issue. Bill Tucker points out that Hemingway drew inspiration for his writing using Cezanne's paintings as an artistic muse (27), a fact that might help some students respect alternative strategies more than they sometimes do. Jacqueline N. Glasgow and Margie S. Bush use a Lego project in a complex project in which students design and build a children's toy out of Legos, write a proposal, instruction manual, and advertising campaign to market it, and then give an oral presentation covering the entire project (32–37). Wendy Simeone has students make original films about such texts as Achebe's *Things Fall Apart* and Wiesel's *Night*. The students' films include "authentic film documentations" spliced into them, along with original dramatizations of the texts and/or musical accompaniment. Some of her students used Japanese dolls in a dramatization of a Japanese myth. She also has students do sketches of American and African proverbs, noting that those who do the best drawings are not always the best writers (60–62). Smagorinsky has good advice about the use of these strategies, relevant to their use at all levels: "The introduction of multiple intelligence activities must be accompanied by large changes in the values of the classroom, and concomitant changes in what students believe to be appropriate and acceptable ways of thinking and communicating in an English class" (25).

Alternate Strategies in College Classes

In my advanced exposition class, I use an exercise similar to Pirie's for *Lord of the Flies* to help students analyze nonfiction texts. In preparation for essays students were going to be writing on "voice," my class was reading essays on "academic" versus "everyday" language, including opinions regarding the "English only" controversy. One day we were discussing separate essays by Richard Rodriguez and Victor Villanueva, anthologized in the *Living Languages* collection (Buffington, Diogenes, and Moneyhun 1997). First I had students write for about five minutes the endings of the following sentences:

In "Aria," Richard Rodriguez argues that . . ."

In "Whose Voice Is It, Anyway?" Victor Villanueva critiques Rodriguez's position on language. Villanueva argues that . . ."

Then I called on people to read the ends of their sentences. This was to establish that everyone more or less understood Rodriguez's and Villanueva's fairly clear—and opposed—positions on bilingual education, "standard" English, and assimilation. As discussed in a previous chapter, Rodriguez sees school English as the key to success, though he acknowledges some loss of connection with family in learning it. Villanueva sees racism as a factor complicating students' assimilation into mainstream society, with or without "proper English." He draws a distinction between "immigrants," people whose ancestors came to America by choice, and "minorities," people whose ancestors did not come by choice or who were colonized. While he sympathizes with some of Rodriguez's anecdotes regarding both the pain and reward of learning English, he takes issue with Rodriguez's view of "standard English" as the key to success for everyone. I should add here that students were not very good at summarizing the two views. Many thought Rodriguez was in favor of bilingual education and that Villanueva agreed with him. Since the issue Rodriguez and Villanueva were debating in print was an important one, especially to ideas of "voice" in student writing, I wanted to do more with these readings, and with the discussion about them, which, given the provocative nature of the Rodriguez/Villanueva written debate, should have been livelier.

The Six-Headed Debate

After the preparation described above, students participated in a "six-headed debate." Here's what we did: I made one half of the room (about eight people) the "Rodriguez side" and the other half the "Villanueva side." First I had students find examples of rhetorical strategies used by their essayist. I gave examples such as Rodriguez calling bilingual education a "scheme" instead of a plan, and using dialogue, family anecdotes, and direct quotations in sections. In Villanueva's piece, there are long, vivid descriptions/analogies about "ethnic" food in supermarkets, showing how much food from immigrants is in the "regular" aisles, but that Mexican food is still in the "ethnic" aisle. He uses this to dispel the analogy of "the melting pot." At one point he says, "No more soup."

Students caught on to this quickly and found other samples of rhetorical strategies. One student pointed out that Rodriguez intersperses Spanish words into his English sentences to show/juxtapose the conflicted emotions he was feeling as he learned "the public language." Another pointed out his depiction of his family's house as a metaphor for how he felt in school: "Our house stood apart—gaudy yellow in a row of white bungalows"(99). Other people found lots of other examples of rhetorical strategies. In addition to providing background reading for essays students were currently writing on "voice," which could be about voice or could demonstrate voice, or both, we were discussing rhetorical strategies partly in preparation for another assignment later in the semester (the rhetorical analysis project discussed in Chapter 3). I find if we do "live" rhetorical analysis in class a bit at a time, students find it easier to do on their own.

That preparatory work took about fifteen minutes. Then I told them that in a few minutes there would be a debate between Richard

Rodriguez and Victor Villanueva, and that they'd have a few minutes to prepare themselves to take part in the debate as Rodriguez or Villanueva. I asked each side to talk in two smaller groups about their writer's main argument, best evidence (metaphors, personal anecdote, statistics, history, etc.), and to anticipate the opponent's argument in order to be ready with a response. They had about five minutes to huddle in this way before the debate.

Then I arranged six chairs in the center of the room: three on one side, and three on the other, facing the other three. Because I was having three "Rodriguezes" facing three "Villanuevas," I selected three people from each side of the room to sit in the six chairs. I told them, "This is a debate on a talk show between Rodriguez and Villanueva. I'm putting three on each side so that you're not up there by yourself." (Although this was a hypothetical debate between only two men, I figured three students on each side would help keep the conversation going, plus it wouldn't put one student on the spot to carry the whole side. They could support each other.) The rest of us watched from an outer circle—the other "Rodriguezes" more or less behind the three in the middle, and the other "Villanuevas" behind their teammates in the center.

This was the statement up for debate: "Learning 'standard' English is the key to success in American society." It took a while to get going. At one point, the Villanueva side was questioning the concept of standard English and what constituted it anyway—that there were so many versions of English, it didn't make sense to insist on one way of speaking. Matt Vaughn, who was a "Rodriguez," then commented on the question in Spanish—which was startling. "Touché," said another student. It instantly demonstrated that someone speaking Spanish in a conventional English classroom might be considered an outsider. Then Anita, also on the Rodriguez side, said that English was the "language of power," but no one picked up that point yet.

The Villanueva side was struggling. They kept restating Villanueva's main point, which was that "immigrants" and "minorities" were different groups from different ancestors, here under different circumstances, and that "standard" English would *not* be a ticket to success for minorities because of racism. But they were not supporting that view with the compelling evidence and examples Villanueva used in his essay.

At this point, I jumped in as a kind of talk-show host: "Professor Villanueva," I began, "you've sometimes spoken of an incident in which as a child you accompanied your father on an apartment-hunting trip. Could you tell us about that?" The Villanuevas quickly skimmed that section of the essay and one of them began, "When I was a boy, I went with my father to find an apartment . . ." (The story is that the apartment owner, thinking that Villanueva and his father were Puerto Ricans, said there were no vacancies. When the father chatted informally with him and said they were from Spain, suddenly there was a vacancy.) The incident supports Villanueva's views that while "minorities" are discriminated against, "immigrants" have a place in the "American Dream," a place to which "minorities" are prevented, by racism, from going. After reading a section of that anecdote, the Villanuevas were able to ad-lib the rest of their response. Then the other side responded, this time with several people wanting to speak at once, and the debate became lively.

I also used this debate in my afternoon class. Again, each side had "coaches" who helped prepare the debaters, but I increased to about fifteen minutes the time they had to do so. As I went between the two groups to help, I realized that some of the Villanueva people completely misunderstood Rodriguez's point. Because Rodriguez starts out saying what a hard time he had and how English interfered with his life with his mother and father, some in this group thought that Rodriguez was in favor of bilingual education. They completely missed how he uses that opening to set the stage for his main argument. It's like he's saying, "Even though I had a hard time and leaving the home language is painful, I'm glad I did because it allowed me to have a public voice." Many readers did not see this as his setup but as his "thesis." They thought the pain he felt learning English was his main point and therefore he was in favor of bilingual education.[4]

The Rodriguez group in the later class seemed to be focusing too much on minorities taking responsibility for learning English, which was *part* of Rodriguez's point, but it seemed to me that this group was not sufficiently addressing Villanueva's distinction between immigrants and minorities. They were not focusing enough on how society views these groups differently, which is key to Villanueva's argument about the role racism plays in some groups being unable to fully assimilate. At that point one of the "coaches" asked if she could jump in, and I said yes. She drew people's attention to a passage later in the essay that clearly articulated the point Rodriguez was building toward, and then the main debaters began referring to passages from the text to support the different views. Both classes flew by. We laughed a lot during this multisensory, participatory, and challenging class, and we discussed serious issues surrounding "standard" English, stereotypes, and racism.

This six-headed debate is not a flawless recipe for great class discussions and wonderfully insightful interpretations. However, it supports several ideas worth emphasizing here. First, all students must literally take a side in an important controversy about language and racism, but taking on the arguments of writers on different sides makes a difficult discussion a bit safer for individuals. Second, the debate draws attention to both essays' powerful rhetorical strategies, which students could now notice in other readings. Being consciously aware of a writer's rhetorical proofs makes readers a little less vulnerable to them. Now that students could see how anecdotes, statistics, or metaphors worked in a persuasive text, they might use them in their own, where appropriate. Third, this debate in the personas of the experts—Rodriguez and Villanueva—also helps students identify with the writers. For a few minutes, they have to speak *as if* they have had the past experiences of either man. It helps them participate in Elbow's "believing game," which asks readers to believe a writer for a while before jumping to instant "doubting" or critique. In this debate, even if someone disagrees with Rodriguez, for example, she has to more or less accurately represent his views as she represents him in the debate.

Finally, this modified "talk-show" debate is multisensory. For those who learn better auditorially, it is a more compelling approach than simply asking students to read paragraphs in an essay. They have to do something orally with what they found. In fact, one person, who had found a good paragraph to use in the debate but had trouble paraphrasing it, said something like, "To illustrate what I mean, I'd like to quote from an article I wrote several years ago on this subject . . ."—and then she read a bit from the book. People laughed, but she did it in a way consistent with the "talk-show" format, and it was effective. This debate forces people used to writing their summaries or comments (in this case mostly English majors or minors) to ad-lib in a dramatic situation. The writers' different views are juxtaposed with every exchange. The debaters have to think fast and articulate as they go—in response to the three people sitting across from them. As is the case with other alternative strategies, it is sometimes surprising which students excel at this kind of intellectual exercise.

Sketching or Mapping a Reading

Since sketching or mapping a draft seemed to give students insights in my writing classes, I decided to use that approach in a graduate course that required much reading. One night in my Composition theory class, a course for all new graduate teaching assistants, I used sketches to help students conceptualize a reading, James Porter's well-known essay, "Intertextuality and the Discourse Community." Giving students about ten minutes, I asked them to draw a visual representation of Porter's critique of traditional Composition theory and practice, as well as his proposed alternate model. To summarize: Porter critiques what he sees as composition textbooks' pervasive, idealized, and romantic view of the original, autonomous text. He argues that all texts are intertexts, comprised of traces of infinite other texts and constrained by specific discourse communities. He says, "readers, not writers, create discourse" (38). By extension, Porter argues, writing pedagogy should not be fo-

Figure 5–1
My drawing of Porter's critique of composition

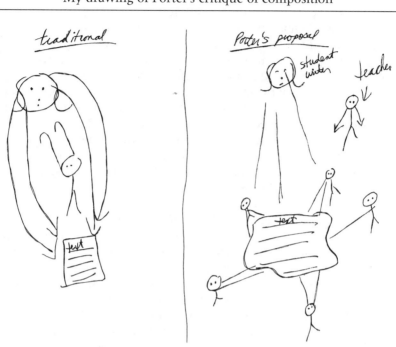

cused, as it is now on prodding the individual writer's brain for original thoughts contained therein, but rather, helping the writer analyze the community at which the text is aimed, the community of readers who ultimately play a large role in shaping the text. "Intertextuality suggests that our goal should be to help students learn to write for the discourse communities they choose to join" (42).

While the students set to work, I produced my own primitive sketch of how I saw traditional conceptions of writer writing, compared to Porter's conception of text being shaped by readers. (See Figure 5–1.)

The sketch shows a teacher standing between the writer and her text, coaxing ideas from the writer's brain, which go directly to a stable, rectangle-shaped text. In this conventional view, the teacher encourages the writer to look within herself for "her ideas," which can then be transferred to her writing. In my sketch of Porter's model, the teacher is still between the writer and her text, but now the teacher is pointing to the many members of the discourse community, who stand around and shape the evolving text. The text is no longer a stable rectangle, but is an amoeba-like amalgam, whose shape shifts as different members of the discourse community push and pull on it. In this model, the teacher's task is to help the student become aware of constraints put on her writing by those others, all of which have a hand, literally, in this sketch, on the writer's text.

After I had put a quick sketch on my paper, I headed to the board in the back of the room to put it up there. I said if anyone else felt like doing so, they could put their sketch on the front or back board, and that there was plenty of chalk, all different colors. I didn't have to ask specific people. Six of the eleven people put their sketches up. This took only about five minutes. We all finished at about the same time, and one by one we explained our models. I must admit that I was excited about my sketch and wanted to go first. Students seemed a bit stunned by this task, but also fascinated and quite engaged. Each person who drew on the board explained his or her work with much animation. As they talked through their visual representation, their explanations of Porter's ideas were lucid and detailed.

Why do something like this? First of all, the act of drawing, like the act of writing, is a heuristic to help them make sense of Porter's important and still radical view of how writing is taught, versus how he thinks it should be taught. When people explain their sketches, they have a visual prop to help them talk through their explanation. Classmates can ask for details and clarification, and everyone gets a number of useful visualizations and metaphors to help them understand Porter's model of writing and pedagogy and to juxtapose it to other models. Each one was different; each used a different format (stick figures, maps, Venn diagram, graphs, and visual metaphors).

If blackboards or whiteboards aren't available, there are other ways to do these visual representations. Students could bring to class, or the instructor could provide, transparencies and markers. They could then explain their sketch on the overhead projector and would not need that five minutes to redraw it on the board. They might use PowerPoint or drawing software; they could show it on a common screen or via a networked system. Or, students could visit individual computer monitors as each artist explains the conceptualization. If nothing else is available, they can use posters or flip charts. While students can do this work at home in preparation for class, I prefer the drama of doing it together, live, as we all grapple with the written texts. People only need 5 to 10 minutes to produce a primitive sketch like the one I did. And then they need only a few minutes each to explain their sketch. It is well worth the time.

Acting out Scenes—A Personal Example

During the last semester of my senior year in college, I took a Shakespeare course from Tom Littlefield, an English professor at SUNY Albany who had a strong interest in drama. He always held his class in an odd-shaped classroom in the basement of the Humanities building, but the room had a small raised platform in the front that could be used as a stage. As an alternative to writing a research paper on a Shakespeare play, he said, we could act out some scenes. We'd have to be familiar with the lines and rehearse. In the class that semester was a drama major, several people like me who had a minor in drama or who had taken some acting classes, and several more people who would do almost anything to avoid another literature paper. We jumped at the chance to "put on a play."

Ultimately, we acted out five scenes taken from Acts IV and V of *Othello*. Gordy, the drama major, directed us. I was Desdemona. We memorized our lines and put together minimum costumes and props, appropriating miscellaneous tables or chairs from the building when we needed them. We rehearsed many nights, on our own time, whenever the classroom was free.

Our director said that in order to speak the lines with some depth, we had to know what every word meant. This involved studying the extended footnotes in the Riverside edition and following up with historical explanations from the *OED*. I never learned as much about a play, the times, or possible interpretations by doing a paper, and I never had more fun in a class. Even now, *Othello* is my favorite play, and I can still remember whole passages from Acts IV and V—not that memorization is the reason for doing Shakespeare. What texts we read and why is something each instructor must work out herself. My point is that my participation in dramatizing a part of a play is my most vivid memory of any class I took in four years of college.

Because that Shakespeare class from my undergraduate days is still so vivid to me, I gave my students at Utica College in an Introduction to Literature class the option of acting out scenes from a play in lieu of writing a paper. One group did an impressive classroom production of *Plumes*, by Georgia Douglas Johnson. They had costumes, props, and had memorized the lines. I could tell from their line delivery that they had discussed the play and the complex social factors that influenced the African American protagonist's agonizing decision not to employ a white doctor to treat her dying daughter. This day happened over five years ago, and it is one of the most memorable classes in my teaching career.

Multi-Modal "Rounds"

I also use alternative formats to help undergraduates connect with difficult readings. In my rhetorical theory class, students have quite a bit of reading to do: the Crowley and Hawhee *Ancient Rhetorics* text, plus a substantial reading packet with complex rhetorical analyses. I knew if we were going to discuss these in class with any depth, students would have to prepare themselves. I designed a series of "rounds," in which students would use oral, written, visual, 3-D, and other modes in which they responded to the readings via overhead sketches of concepts, voice-mail responses, e-mailed journal entries, peer responses to those entries, as well as oral presentations of some kind. These responses would count as 20 percent of the course grade, and each person had a chance to respond in each of five different formats. In each round:

- five people do an oral reading log (a 1- to 2-minute call to my voice mail before class).
- five people write a 250-word e-mail to me, cc to class.
- five people write a brief e-mail response to those five, and copies to the class and to me.
- five people prepare an overhead transparency. This is a drawn, sketched, or graphed response to the reading(s) of the day. It should be completed before class with a fine-point, wet-erase marker on one sheet of overhead projector film, which the student should be prepared to place on the overhead and explain/discuss with the class.
- five people prepare a 3-D response. This is a 5- to 15-minute response that may be one of a number of things: a declamation, a debate, a Greek fashion show, a skit, a scene, a dialogue, a sculpture, a 3-D model, a dance, a song, a relevant game, and so on.

The rounds generated many kinds of responses, different in quality and in approach. For one of the "3-D" presentations, there was a "Who Wants to Be a Millionaire?"–style game show using definition-type questions from the Crowley and Hawhee text—providing us with a simple but surprisingly riveting testing of words such as *kairos, ethos, enargeia, commonplace, epideictic,* etc. This game obviously did not involve analytical thinking, but it was a dramatic and participatory review of terms useful for students of rhetoric to have at their fingertips. Derek used pre-made signs in an interesting sketch to show how metaphors are used in technical writing. He was able to show how what we were reading in our class was different from, but related to, rhetorical work in technical writing classes. Someone else did a rhetorical analysis of letters to the editor in the college newspaper, followed days later by someone else doing a rhetorical analysis of an *Amistad*-related debate going on in the e-mailed portion of the rounds. That is, one student led the class in a discussion of rhetorical strategies used in her classmate's e-mailed comments about an issue we had been discussing in class. I held my breath during this presentation, hoping the writer of the e-mail argument would not take offense. She seemed to enjoy it, however, and helped analyze her own words and phrases.

In another e-mailed entry, part of the "rounds" assignment, one student took a suggestion from the text to experiment with grammatical person—switching a paragraph from third person to "I" or "you"—and discuss the effect of the change. She chose some well-known advertising slogans and discussed the rhetorical effects of changing, for example, "You're in good hands with Allstate," to "I'm in good hands . . . ," or "We're in good hands," or "They're in good hands." We also wrote online about subtle rhetorical differences in altered versions of the "Just do it" Nike slogan:

"I just do it."

"People just do it."

"You just do it."

This was a written discussion, but it took place outside of class time via e-mail to everyone in the class, which they could read at times most convenient to them.

Ellen and Keri did a joint presentation on commonplaces. They wrote bumper-sticker sayings on the board, the first one from Teresa, who gave them, "I love my country but fear my government." They discussed ideologies reflected in that statement and in another one that came from the class, "Charleton Heston is my president." Keri put on a reference to lyrics from the music group Phish: "Tires are the things on the car that make contact with the road." The subsequent discussion they led established the importance of context, intertextuality, and kairotic elements necessary for bumper-sticker readers to understand the Charleton Heston reference as well as the allusion to the Phish lyrics.

Nancy used her turn at the overhead transparency to demonstrate stasis theory. The top panel, with a smiling face on the right side, shows people disagreeing about living wills, but they are in stasis. (See Figure 5–2.) That is, they agree on what it is, exactly, that they disagree about:

"I choose not to suffer."

"You shouldn't have a right to choose."

In contrast, Nancy's bottom panel shows two groups of people carrying placards and yelling things at each other. The unhappy face depicted on the right indicates that the groups have not reached stasis: there is "no agreement on the disagreement." Nancy used the overhead to discuss more complex examples of stasis theory from the Crowley and Hawhee text. For people having trouble with the readings, and several people indicated on their voice-mail or e-mail comments that

Figure 5–2
Arguers reaching, then failing to reach, stasis

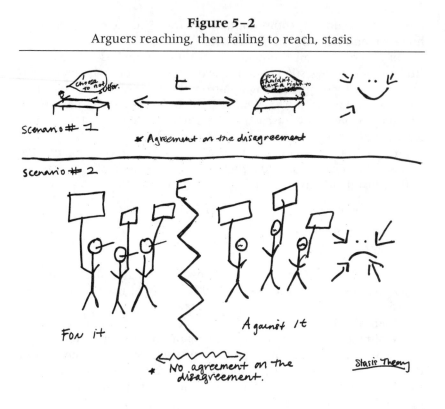

they were, Nancy's visual depiction of stasis and lack-of-stasis provided a good point of departure for class discussion. She showed that people setting out to discuss euthanasia who begin by saying, "Euthanasia should be (should not be) legal" would immediately need to address questions of definition.

For her overhead presentation, Teresa did a simple but effective transparency showing how visual rhetoric could be used to dramatize the AIDS epidemic in Africa. In each box on the right side, in red, is the symbol for AIDS research. The top left box has minimalist drawings of a mother, father, and child. The next box shows the father gone. He is dead from AIDS. The next panel shows the mother gone, with only the orphan remaining. The last panel shows only a grave. The child has also succumbed to the epidemic. (See Figure 5–3.)

Teresa's sketch showed the power of visual rhetoric and the stark reality of what AIDS is doing to families in Africa. She discussed how complex explanations of the epidemic or lists of statistics might be enhanced rhetorically by a minimalist drawing.

In the same rhetoric theory class, we also used sketches routinely in class work to help students contrast epistemological differences be-

Figure 5-3
Visual rhetoric to underscore the AIDS crisis in Africa

tween ancient and modern rhetorics or to represent concepts in some of the complex readings we were doing. We also used sketches midway through a long analysis project as a way for students to step back from their drafts to see if they were happy with the framework (see Elizabeth's in Chapter 3).

Sketches on the Final Exam

Interestingly, on the final exam in this course, two students used unsolicited sketches to enhance their written answers. Writing about Jane Tompkin's critique of what is conventionally valued in American literary criticism, one student illustrated the status of different texts in the literary canon (Shakespeare's versus Harriet Beecher Stowe's). Here is the question Robert was answering:

> Relate Jane Tompkins's argument about literary history to Jeanne Fahnestock's and Marie Secor's argument about literary history and epideictic rhetoric. How do these views regarding the reception of certain texts as "literature" impact the reception of Harriet Beecher Stowe's novel *Uncle Tom's Cabin*? Discuss another literary text you know about and explain how it does or does not fit the "shared criteria" Fahnestock and Secor say appear to be important in the literary criticism they read from 1978–1982. Why does any of this matter?

Here's what Robert wrote in answer to question #2. The brackets indicate the handwritten portion I could not make out.

> Jane Tompkins and Fahnestock are related to each other in their seemingly overall view of literary history. Both works seem to suggest that it revolves around who literature caters to and who sets the criteria.
>
> In both works, the authors are showing how those who held the power set the outcome for the literary circle. This to them is wrong and these paradigms need to be redefined and understood in a different light.
>
> In Fahnestock and Secor, the two authors simply tear apart the idea of literary criticism. To them, it is a waste of time and simply is a group who defines what's good and bad. The question remains, what is the criteria for this? Simply because one book or text is better for discussion does not make it a better piece of work. This is what literary criticism and history is about; these books can be discussed, torn apart, and rediscovered for the profile. So, when Tompkins talks about a book that has "sentimental power," it could never fit this category?!
>
> This is how they all relate: the idea of a need to revise how we look, judge, and set criteria in the literary world. For example, on p. 175 Tompkins states that the idea of the literary circle not being able to accept a work like Uncle Tom's Cabin is because of how [?] defines the terms. As Oravec says, these also define the terms in the argument. In this case, a book that holds no argument purpose can not be of value. This is wrong and when authors are arguing for a revision in the way literary circles are judged.
>
> If those who set the criteria redefined how books are judged, a book like Uncle Tom's Cabin would move into the literary canon. In my picture [that] I drew for the Tompkins piece, I drew something similar to this. (See Figure 5–4.)

Figure 5–4

An exam sketch of the canon controversy; Shakespeare in the "clouds" of the canon; *Uncle Tom's Cabin* in the "cellar"

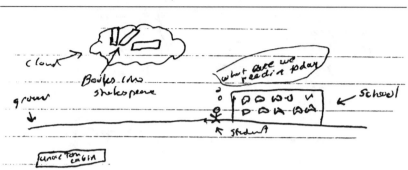

In Robert's sketch, a stick-figure student is at a school asking, "What are we reading today?" Meanwhile, the book *Uncle Tom's Cabin* is below a sketched line, relegated to the "cellar," under a cloud filled with "books on Shakespeare." Here is how Robert describes his sketch:

> In this picture, for a book like Uncle Tom's Cabin to move out of the cellar and reach the clouds (the literary canon), the idea of how things are defined and the criteria must be reevaluated! Those who define the terms of engagement win.
>
> I think that all the articles that we have read somewhat tie together with the works of Fahnestock and Secor. They all establish that how we define the terms and who sets these terms or [?] have the "trump card" and will hold the power. The work of Sharon Crowley holds true to this statement. She looks at "taste" and how it is the group who hold the literary values and do not seem to feel anyone out or away from their "taste" is worth anything. Once again, these [?] set the terms, define them, and get the [?] hold all the power.
>
> The same holds true with the works by Oravec and even Corder. Corder for example said in the literary circles argument—passed over what is looked at and viewed. As Oravec would say, it is all in who defines the terms.
>
> It all matters because with all these arguments they hope to use rhetoric as the key to promoting change in the higher powers who set the criteria. For rhetoric is used all the time, regardless if you know it or not, and [through] it arguments about issues are made. Thus, the works that we have read all encourage rhetorical usage to make changes in those that are not right such as criteria and literary circles that define terms. In fact, they all seem to hold the common thread of criteria and invoking change in how this criteria for things is set.

Another student, Kim, also used a sketch to explain her answer on the final. She was addressing this question: "Explain Jacqueline Jones

Figure 5–5
An exam sketch showing positive effects of Royster's proposal

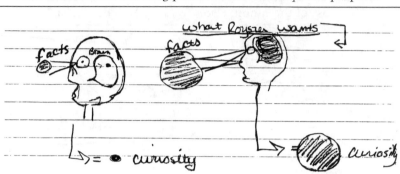

Royster's dissatisfaction with 'mainstream public discourses.' What does she propose as a way to address problems with public discourses? If her plan is successful, what differences might we see in public discourses of the future?" She drew a diagram to help her represent Jacqueline Jones Royster's critique of the public reception of the film *Amistad*. In Kim's sketch, she juxtaposes the way things are now (on the left) with the re-form Royster is suggesting (on the right). In the left sketch, a person's brain is exposed to a small circle of facts, and as a result has a small amount of curiosity. (See Figure 5–5.)

In the "What Royster wants" side of the sketch, a person is exposed to a circle of facts about five times as large as the one on the left, and as a result, the person's "curiosity" is proportionately larger. I think the sketch provided a better explanation than her written answer:

> The mainstream public discourses most likely keeps it [its] attention to the popular (majority) which is white Americans. For example, this would also be middle class. This is the material that is being accepted into a social canon. Royster believes we should begin to "produce thick descriptions" of people. For example a single quote cannot just be looked at from someone but the quotes and words before and after the quote. This will open rhetoric to more reality and truth because there will be more experience and information available about the searcher and the one being searched. There will be more to werk [sic] with so that the audience will be perusaded using rhetorical techniques. This would be benefitial [sic] for everyone. With more information to be learned there will be more to be read and watched. Im [sic] having a hard time putting this into werds [sic] so here is a diagram to help you understand more.

Kim answered this question last, so perhaps she was running out of time. Her written answer has a number of surface errors. They are not typos, for this was handwritten. She does not include an explanation of the sketch, perhaps because of time constraints. I do think, however, it represents her answer better than her written account. It is in the sketch that she suggests that a reader's "curiosity" will be expanded by reading fuller accounts of "thick description."

These students' unsolicited use of sketches or diagrams to enhance their written answers could simply be due to their wish to impress a teacher they know encourages different representations. I prefer to think, of course, that sketches helped them with their papers earlier in the semester, and they used them on the final to help them discover or articulate their views.

Using alternative formats, multiple channels, or various intelligences to help our students (and ourselves) obtain broader, more complex conceptualizations of issues is an idea we should all investigate further. We must anticipate objections to such intellectual work, however, and be prepared to handle questions about it. As mentioned early in this chapter, Peter Smagorinsky, Bruce Pirie, and others who experimented with unconventional projects encountered skepticism from their colleagues, who doubted that these multisensory projects counted as "real" learning. Stephen North, too, acknowledged that performance pieces run the risk of being seen by some as "unserious/gimmicky/not what one espects from 'real intellectuals'" (191). This doubting may be even more prevalent in English departments at colleges and universities, where professors are judged less on their performance as teachers and more on the written texts they publish. How those of us who wish to experiment with alternate pedagogies might address this skepticism in our professional lives is addressed in the next chapter.

Notes

1. In workshops I attended that Barbara Walvoord gave at Utica College in the early 1990s, she used a version of these questions.

2. See especially pages 73–77 of his book for a more complete description of the fusion model.

3. Pirie credits inspiration for these multisensory activities to these and other books:

Boal, Augusto. *Games for Actors and Non-Actors.* Translated by Adrian Jackson. New York: Routledge, 1992.

Blom, Lynne Anne, and L. Tarin Chaplin. *The Moment of Movement: Dance Improvisation.* Pittsburgh: University of Pittsburgh Press, 1988.

Wagner, Betty Jane. *Dorothy Heathcote: Drama as a Learning Medium.* London: Hutchinson, 1979.

4. This is not the first time I've seen students misread an article when the writer spends the first few paragraphs summarizing the debate or beginning with the other side. I think this is because many students have been programmed to think in five-paragraph-theme format: the thesis must come first, followed by support. They have trouble reading essays that depart from that formula—which are most essays. For a further discussion of this phenomenon, see my "Marginal Comments on Writers' Texts: The Status of the Commenter as a Factor in Writing Center Tutorials," in *Stories from the Center: Connecting Narrative and Theory in the Writing Center,* edited by Lynn Craigue Briggs and Meg Woolbright, 31–42. Urbana, IL: NCTE, 2000.

Chapter Six

Handling Professional Issues

Much Madness is divinest Sense—
To a discerning Eye—
Much Sense—the starkest Madness—
'Tis the Majority
In this, as All prevail—
Assent—and you are sane—
Demur—you're straightway dangerous—
And handled with a Chain—

—Emily Dickinson

John Mayher, in *Uncommon Sense: Theoretical Practice in Language Education,* critiques the common perception among students, teachers, parents, and the general public that "real" learning must be both boring and difficult, not fun: "The common sense equation seems to be that if it's painful, it's productive; if it's fun, it's trivial and a waste of time" (52). Most of the recommendations discussed so far in this book are controversial for reasons Mayher discusses. Instructors who consider incorporating the spirit of these strategies into their own pedagogy must come to terms with them both practically and philosophically. They may have to defend to students, colleagues, administrators, the general public, or even to themselves, their supplementing of print-based methodologies with "multiple channel" alternatives.

As we saw in the last chapter, Bruce Pirie and Peter Smagorinsky, who contributed two articles in the special multiple-intelligence issue of *English Journal*, each had to address skeptical or dismissive comments from colleagues. Stephen North also recognized the risk that the "performance practices" his students created may be viewed as "gimmicky" (2000, 191). Indeed, it is easy to find such skepticism, as well as "common sense" assumptions about intelligence and what constitutes "real" learning in professional journals as well as in the mainstream media. This chapter will help prepare those committed to using multiple literacies for typical reactions to their use. It will suggest ways to frame the issue for students, colleagues, and administrators.

Reactions to Multiple Literacies in the Academic and Commercial Print Media

Reactions to the *English Journal* multiple-intelligence issue described in the last chapter continued for two months after it was published. As Linda Hecker points out, those letters to the editor, both supportive and critical of the strategies described, provide a good overview of disagreements regarding learning (46). Four of the five letters are generally supportive of the practices described in the issue. In his lengthy letter, however, Alan Pierpoint critiques Gardner's multiple intelligence theory as an excuse teachers can use for not holding "today's youth accountable for the demands of print literacy." He says, "The picture is easier than the essay," and that "non-verbal assignments" do not do "the serious work" of an English class, which is to "teach writing" (12). What is interesting here is not Pierpoint's objection to multiple intelligence theory, but his assumption that writing is "the serious work" of an English class, and apparently essay-related work is the only way to "teach writing." He seems to assume readers hold the same definitions of *writing* he does, limiting it to only those intellectual conceptualizations that can be rendered in print. His easy juxtapositioning of the "picture" as being "easier" than the essay, his conviction that only the essay can "do the serious work" of English and fulfill the "demands" of "print literacy," reveal his unquestioning acceptance of literacy commonplaces.

He is not alone. As bell hooks points out, few reformers of higher education have taken a serious look at the role "fun" or "pleasure" might play in higher education. She says, *"Excitement* in higher education was viewed as potentially disruptive of the atmosphere of seriousness assumed to be essential to the learning process" (her emphasis, 1994, 7). She argues later in *Teaching to Transgress* that instructors may not experiment with innovative strategies because of what their own students might think: "I think our fear of losing students' respect has discouraged many professors from trying new teaching practices" (145).

Multi-modal strategies are easily ridiculed. In her essay in the *English Journal* M-I issue, Barbara Osburg is mostly arguing against ranking and assessing students, but she takes a cheap shot: "And if we want to know if a kid can do algebra, he's still got to work a problem, not sing a song about π" (14), as if anyone had seriously suggested that. In a cartoon by Kerry Soper in *The Chronicle of Higher Education,* one of twelve panels depicting "Things You Shouldn't Say at Your Dissertation Defense" has a candidate saying to his committee: "This morning I decided to trash the written version and communicate the sum of my work through interpretive dance" (B11). These jokes work because they misrepresent and extremize multi-modal strategies, and they imply that these activities will completely take the place of written work. They also rely on readers' shared assumptions and unquestioned ideologies concerning the superiority of print literacy.

Unquestioned ideologies are everywhere in general-interest magazines. In an essay entitled "Dumb and Dumber," the editors of *U.S. News and World Report* point to "fresh evidence" social critics cite as indicators of a downward intelligence slide in the United States:

> New York recently found that more than half of its fourth graders flunked standard English. In Massachusetts, 43 percent of teachers failed performance tests. Among Americans under age 30, nearly half get their political news from the late-night talk shows. And so it goes. (20)

It would take an entire chapter to respond adequately to this string of "evidence," and to be fair, the editors later acknowledged recent American Nobel prize–winners and successes in business and industry. They use these three sentences mostly as an attention-getter to their essay, which is subtitled, "An invitation to a dialogue on America's intellectual capacity."

The assumptions in the editorial supporting those three sentences, however, are not up for debate. First, flunking "standard English" (no scare quotes in their use of those terms) is seen as unquestioned proof of New York's fourth graders' stupidity. The implied binary goes like this: "If you can speak standard English, you're smart. If you can't, you're dumb." There is not even a whiff of a reference to all the research that long ago debunked the commonplace that mastery of "standard English" is an indicator of intelligence (Labov 1966; Smitherman 1999; Gilyard 1996b). Second, if 43 percent of Massachusetts' teachers failed "performance tests," it must be the teachers who are "dumb," never the "performance tests," which control the "smart/dumb" judgment instantly applied by pundits. The third piece of "fresh evidence" that Americans under thirty are getting "dumber" is that "nearly half get their political news from the late-night talk shows." The assumption here seems to be that anything that appears in the print medium must by definition be more sophisticated than anything on television.

Public whinings about literacy frequently also rely on, and demonstrate, binary thinking. Syndicated columnist Kathleen Parker rips into a pilot program being used at nine colleges to test students' spatial talents, as demonstrated with Legos, as part of their college entrance exam. Her column title, "Legos Test: Wrong Way to Decide Who Goes to College" assumes a "right" way to make that decision, and Parker is simplistically sure about what belongs in that category. Knowledge, for her, is like an on/off toggle switch: "You either can read or you can't; you either can do math or you can't. That's about as simple as it gets" (2000, A8).

Similarly, Cal Thomas begins his column supporting home schooling with a simplistic declaration: "The top three finishers in last week's National Spelling Bee are educated at home." This fact is apparently self-evident proof of the superiority of home schooling—that good spellers have acquired the "real knowledge and the endangered species known as wisdom" that Thomas sees lacking in the "dumbed-down" public schools (A13). He feels no need to defend good spelling as an indicator of superiority, relying instead on his readers' shared beliefs that this "real knowledge" speaks for itself.

As Mike Rose points out in *Lives on the Boundary*, complaints about illiteracy are not new and should be put in context. He notes that the president of Brown University complained in 1841 that "students frequently enter college almost wholly unacquainted with English grammar." Similarly, a Harvard professor claimed that some graduates produced "manuscripts [that] would disgrace a boy of twelve" (cited by Rose 1989, 5). This was in the 1870s. Rose's quotations of similar whining continue for two more pages, during which he also points out that definitions of "functional illiteracy" have changed numerous times throughout the twentieth century.[1]

Rose does not deny that schools have problems, but his point is that post-lapsarian laments—complaints about how great the past used to be and how terrible things are now—have been, and continue to be, conventional reactions to the behavior of young people by older ones. Of course some students *are* failing in school. "But if you can get close enough to their failure," Rose argues, "you'll find knowledge that the assignment didn't tap, ineffective rules and strategies that have a logic of their own; you'll find clues, as well, to the complex ties between literacy and culture, to the tremendous difficulties our children face as they attempt to find their places in the American educational system" (8).

However, the uninformed assumptions and critiques demonstrated in the media quotations above crystallize important issues, forcing us to ask ourselves these questions:

- What are we doing when we teach writing or analyze texts?
- Why are we doing it?
- Whose interests does it serve?
- What social, intellectual, or physical processes does writing (or thinking) involve for us and for our students?

We should raise these questions publicly also. We should challenge pundits on their narrow views of knowledge, learning, and people.

Initiating Criticism

One option to deflecting criticism for using multisensory strategies is to take a more proactive stance, to point to the limits of traditional approaches: the linguistic-oriented few who are privileged in such a system; the lost insights of those excluded; the discriminatory nature of print-heavy pedagogies. For those who like studies, there is a disturbing one in a 1992 *Gifted Child Quarterly* that found teachers expected students "with verbal, analytic, and social abilities" to be more successful than students with "motor and creative arts" abilities (Guskin, Peng, and Simon, 34). Such expectations may make "common sense" in a system that rewards abilities listed in the first set and ignores those in the second. These findings are more chilling, however, when we consider that students who are expected to succeed usually succeed, and those who are expected to fail usually fail. Overcoming "common sense" expectations may be nearly impossible. But we should try to be consciously aware of our expectations for individual students, based as they probably are on our perceptions of a limited selection of abilities. If we are at least aware of the judgments we are making, we may postpone them long enough to allow students' other talents to come to the fore so that they can use them in pursuit of whatever intellectual work we expect them to do in our classes.

Defining Terms

In addition to raising questions about the overuse of text-based pedagogies, those committed to using multiple channels should pay attention to another important professional issue: the definition of terms. Whose terms are used in discussions about how to teach writing or other courses in English? Who gets to frame any arguments concerning the issue?

Mary Minock initiated discussions of a writing-across-the-curriculum program at her institution by posing key terms for her colleagues to discuss and define. She explains that this process helped open conversations with colleagues who held different views of writing and learning. She began by focusing on the common terms "audience," "self," "context," and "community" to help "work toward a rhetorical estimation of our differences" (510). Similarly, we might respond to, or begin, conversations about multi-modal strategies by opening up definitions of "writing," "reading," "text," or other terms relevant to literacy discussions. We might find that while we in Composition think of "writing" as a complex of activities, intellectual processes, and perspective jolts leading up to and including a drafted product, our colleagues think of "writing" as the dressed up "expression" of the "content" they teach, or worse, the surface niceties of style, or cosmetics of copy editing. Trying to define "writing" jointly, or at least discovering where our conceptions differ, might be a good place to begin.

It is also important to define relevant terms with our students. Addressing bald claims about writing and literacy that appear in the media might be a good way to begin. Twenty years ago, C. H. Knoblauch and Lil Brannon advised teachers to "define [their] commenting vocabularies" when writing on student papers (1981, 1). Such advice might be extended to encourage negotiated definitions of terms brought up in class ("writing," "reading," "grammar," "correctness," etc.) as well as the historical context supporting different constructions of those terms. Students deserve to be privy to underlying reasons their classes are the way they are. Then they can make informed decisions to support or reject those reasons and to negotiate course design. We need to help students deconstruct epistemological assumptions behind word-based pedagogies and whose interests these pedagogies serve. Students need to talk about theory. They need to see theory at work in classroom practice and vice versa. Louise Phelps advises discussing theory with students: "It seems to me inevitable that a teacher should introduce Theory, in the sense of formal, focalized knowledge about discourse, to students; there is no way to avoid it other than utter silence" (234).

Joining Public Debate

Most importantly, we need to make our voices heard in public discussions of literacy, which are usually of the post-lapsarian lament variety described above. Pundits should be challenged on blithe uses of the phrase "standard English," on naive assumptions about "performance tests," on extremized and ridiculous examples of multisensory strategies. They should also be called on the apparent, and usually limited, definition of the terms they use.

Rhetoricians Michael Bruner and Max Oelschlaeger argue that definitions are everything in a public debate. In critiquing the "owls versus people" false dichotomy that environmentalists need to overcome, Bruner and Oelschlaeger write: "Our point is simple: *whoever defines the terms of the public debate determines its outcomes*" (their emphasis 218). Therefore, if uninformed readers of syndicated columns believe, as the columnists seem to, that "writing" means conformity to "standard English" and "grammar rules," it is up to us to call those terms and phrases into question, using the studies and arguments discussed in earlier chapters of this book and elsewhere. But we must choose rhetorical proofs appropriate to the readers of the particular forum in which the column or article appeared. In fact, figuring out how to make such arguments might be projects worthy of courses in writing or rhetoric.

Designing such context-specific projects with students is one way to address the real or imagined "epidemic" of cheating and plagiarism "sweeping through our schools" (for example, see the cover story in *U. S. News & World Report,* November 22, 1999). If a writing assignment is designed anew each semester, finding it in an online research paper catalog becomes increasingly difficult. If the assignment is performance-based, it is impossible.

Taking advantage of the ongoing and escalating panic regarding plagiarism is another way we might proactively address issues of writing, literacy, and alternate strategies before they are framed in someone else's terms. Coming at these issues through public debates of the plagiarism "epidemic" might accomplish two things. It would draw attention to the over-emphasis of print-based literacy, and it would create openings for multiple-channel projects because they are, at least for now, off-the-wall enough not to be found in term paper mills.

Protecting Precious Print

In *Standing in the Shadow of Giants: Plagiarists, Authors, Collaborators,* Rebecca Moore Howard argues that "patchwriting" (almost word-for-word copying with a few changes) is something many academics practice with impunity, or are rewarded for through frequent publications. Yet, when students do it, they can be expelled for "cheating" or "plagiarism." Here I want to bracket my reservations about the breadth of her claim, though I agree with the essence of her argument, in order to address another point she makes. Howard says calling patchwriting cheating "serves liberal culture gatekeeping purposes: it is a means of determining who is *already possessed* of high literacy. It brands those who are still acquiring high literacy not as learners but as criminals, thereby fettering their acquisition of high literacy" (her emphasis xxii). I would like to extend her point a bit by arguing that obsessive attention to the letter of the plagiarism law (which I must admit I have been guilty of) overemphasizes print literacy, at the same time it undervalues other literacies. Instead of deflecting self-righteous critiques in the popular media concerning our alleged capitulation to student plagiarists, we should transform the plagiarism "crisis" into an opportunity to question limited conceptions of "literacy."

Asking Questions

Before critics or colleagues find fault with our use of multiple-channel approaches, we should ask them why they're still supporting conventional term papers. Almost twenty years ago in *College English*, Richard Larson argued against using "the research paper" in composition courses, calling it "a non-form of writing" (1982, 811). There is simply no excuse for assigning "research papers" so unoriginally conceived that they can be cycled and recyled, cut and pasted ad nauseum. In contrast, projects that demand a one-time mix of oral, social, spatial, written, and/or performative work would be impossible to download. What's more, by combining such approaches, students would more nearly anticipate the variety of intellectual work they will undoubtedly need to do in their future professions: collaborating with others, negotiating web space, giving presentations, sketching or creating charts or graphs, as well as writing. So why is writing still so exclusively celebrated and protected? Let others explain their choices.

Embracing Research Critically

There is much we do not know about how multiple talents might work to enhance writing pedagogy. We need, therefore, to look beyond Composition for relevant research. As many have pointed out, Composition began in a spirit of inclusiveness, of an openness to research from other disciplines. In some ways it continues that tradition, but for a variety of reasons, sometimes good ones, it has restricted what research it will incorporate and what research it won't. While I'm not advocating that all research be embraced, I think Composition can be more forgiving of research paradigms that might conflict with ours. It's possible to think about research that might have implications for our students, even if we have qualms about researchers' apparent assumptions.[2]

For example, John Reece and Geoff Cumming cite research by Gould, Conti, and Hovanyecz from the early 1980s that investigated writing done by people using "the listening typewriter."[3] In this ingenious experiment, which took place well before the current explosion of high-quality speech-recognition technology, a typist sat behind a computer screen while a "writer" spoke to the computer. This allowed the text to appear on the screen, simulating contemporary speech-to-screen programs. Researchers compared the resulting texts to those produced through other writing and dictation methods, and found the writing to be "generally superior" to that produced by other writing or dictation methods. Reece and Cumming say little about what constituted a "superior" judgment. However, as Charles Lowe pointed out in his CCCC 2000 presentation, this and similar research is rare in Composition, which should be—but is not—eager to study these results and design updated versions of these experiments.

Familiar But Ignored Calls for Broad-Based Research

In her discussion of the "inner-directed" and "outer-directed" theoretical schools that comprise Composition (referred to in Chapter 1), Patricia Bizzell in *Academic Discourse and Critical Consciousness* calls for broad-based research: "Answers to what we need to know about writing will have to come from both the inner-directed and the outer-directed theoretical schools if we wish to have a complete picture of the composing process. We need to explain the cognitive and the social factors in writing development, and even more important, the relationship between them" (1992, 81–82). Peter Elbow has long recommended "embracing contraries," and Stephen M. North has said that if Composition is to continue as a healthy field, its members should first develop a "heightened methodological consciousness," and second that "All methods and all kinds of knowledge, would have to be assumed to be created equal" (1987, 370–71).

Recent Calls for Changes in Research Design and Purpose

More recently, Davida Charney has argued that empirical research has been essentialized and too readily dismissed: "Our over-reliance on qualitative studies and repeated disparagement of objective methods is creating a serious imbalance in studies of technical and professional writing—and the same may be true in composition as a whole" (589–90). Ellen Barton, too, has pointed out the potential harm done by too-easy dismissals of other people's research. She criticizes "the field's ethical turn [which] appears to have left other methodologies behind, especially those that do not foreground collaborative research relationships and self-reflexive personae" (402). She views as harmful what she sees as Composition's proclivity for "arguing negatively against other methodologies" (401). Ruth Ray and Ellen Barton call for a comprehensive reconsideration of whose interests research should serve. When doing research on writing in nursing homes and rhetorical analyses on disabilities, Ray and Barton discovered, respectively, that they had to overturn their initial assumptions: "We had to re-define our ethical commitments to these communities not in our terms but in theirs" (214).

In looking for ways to reconceive writing-across-the-curriculum (WAC) theory and practice, Elizabeth A. Flynn, Kathryn Remlinger, and William Bulleit have recommended an "interactivity" theory relevant to discussions of multiple channel use:

> Interactional approaches to WAC, though, emphasize writing as a social and political process as well as an individual one and see writers as able to alter discourse communities rather than merely adjust to them. They become potential agents of political and social transformation. (360)

Similarly, an interactional approach to teaching writing or textual studies would emphasize each student's way of making knowledge at the same time see each student using that now-respected knowledge to make changes in the status quo.

Finally, James Thomas Zebroski describes a comprehensive "theory of theory," that would avoid dichotomies and hierarchies and focus instead on an "ecology of practices" that "integrates an understanding of a large number of practices, and the communities which attend to them, into a tolerant, but not eclectic, theory" (1998, 43–44). Interestingly, he uses sketches and diagrams to explain his theory.

Universal Design

Perhaps the most intriguing model with which to frame a commitment to multiple, alternate strategies comes from outside our field. "Universal design" is an architecture-related concept also employed in other areas of design. The idea behind universal design, as Roberta Null explains, is "to redesign the built world—its interiors, exteriors, products, and furnishings—so that it will be usable for all people" (Null and Cherry 1998, ix). This concept provides an apt parallel, and a kairotic moment, for the argument in this book: what is important is not so much the products themselves but the ideology behind the design, just as the few strategies described here are important not for the activities themselves but for the change in perspective their description might inspire. Here is Null on the importance of changing worldview:

> The universal design process is not just the methodological design of building a house or tinkering with a few specifications to make a slightly different version of an existing environment. Universal design asks for the design of an entirely new creature. Designers are being asked to embrace the chaos of discovery, to put imagination before skill—and in the process to re-create the world. (1998, 47)

Using multiple-channel strategies requires that all of us likewise "embrace the chaos of discovery": teacher/theorists and their students as they design and complete multi-modal projects, and colleagues, administrators, and critics as they learn to understand theoretically, and then embrace, the "new creature" that emerges.

Using the productive chaos of multiple-channel literacies will help us rethink our purposes, broaden our epistemological assumptions, and refresh the methodologies supporting them. It will force us to have greater expectations for ourselves and for all our students.

Notes

1. According to Rose, in the 1930s, "having three or more years of schooling" was equated with "functional literacy." These three years were increased to five, then six, then eight, and then to the finishing of the twelfth grade (6).

2. See especially pages 188–94 in *Learning Re-Abled* for a discussion of such research.

3. I am grateful to Charles Lowe for his reference to this research in his CCCC 2000 presentation.

Works Cited

Anson, C. M. 1989. *Writing and Response: Theory, Practice, and Research.* Urbana, IL: NCTE.

Aronowitz, S. 1993. "Paulo Freire's Radical Democratic Humanism." In *Paulo Freire: A Critical Encounter,* eds. P. McLaren and P. Leonard, 8–24. London and New York: Routledge.

Barndt, D. 1998. "The World in a Tomato: Revising the Use of 'Codes' in Freire's Problem-Posing Education." *Convergence* tribute to Paulo Freire, (1 & 2): 62–73.

Barrs, M. 1988. "Drawing a Story: Transitions Between Drawing and Writing." In *The Word for Teaching Is Learning: Essays for James Britton,* eds. M. Lightfoot and N. Martin, 51–69. Portsmouth, NH: Heinemann.

Barton, E. 2000. "More Methodological Matters: Against Negative Argumentation." *College Composition and Communication* 51 (3): 399–416.

Beach, R. 1989. "Showing Students How to Assess: Demonstrating Techniques for Response in the Writing Conference." In *Writing and Response: Theory, Practice, and Research,* ed. C. M. Anson, 127–48. Urbana, IL: NCTE.

Belenky, M. F., B. M. Clinchy, N. R. Goldberger, & J. M. Tarule. 1986. *Women's Ways of Knowing: Development of Self, Voice, and Mind.* New York: Basic Books.

Berkenkotter, C., & T. N. Huckin. 1995. "Gatekeeping at an Academic Convention." In *Genre Knowledge in Disciplinary Communication: Cognition/Culture/Power,* 97–116. Hillsdale, NJ: Lawrence Erlbaum Associates.

Berlin, J. A. 1982. "Contemporary Composition: The Major Pedagogical Theories." *College English* 44 (8) (December): 765–77. In *Cross-Talk in Comp Theory,* ed. V. Villanueva, 233–48. Urbana, IL: NCTE

———. 1988. "Rhetoric and Ideology in the Writing Class." *College English* 50 (5) (September): 477–94. In *Cross-Talk in Comp Theory: A Reader,* ed. V. Villanueva, 679–99. Urbana, IL: NCTE.

———. 1996. *Rhetorics, Poetics, and Cultures: Refiguring College English Studies.* Urbana, IL: NCTE.

Berthoff, A. E. 1981. *The Making of Meaning: Metaphors, Models, and Maxims for Writing Teachers.* Upper Montclair, NJ: Boynton/Cook.

———. 1984. *Reclaiming the Imagination: Philosophical Perspectives for Writers and Teachers of Writing.* Portsmouth, NH: Boynton/Cook.

———. 1990. "'Reading the World . . . Reading the Word': Paulo Freire's Pedagogy of Knowing." In *The Sense of Learning*, ed. A. Berthoff, 114–26. Portsmouth, NH: Boynton/Cook.

———. 1997. "Remembering Paulo Freire." *JAC* 17(3): 305–10.

Bizzell, P. 1982. "Cognition, Convention, and Certainty: What We Need to Know About Writing." *PRE/TEXT* 3 (3): 213–43. In *Cross-Talk in Comp Theory*, ed. V. Villanueva, 365–89. Urbana, IL: NCTE.

———. 1984. "William Perry and Liberal Education." *College English* 46.5 (September): 447–454. In *Academic Discourse and Critical Consciousness*. Pittsburgh and London: University of Pittsburgh Press (1992): 153–63. In *Cross-Talk in Comp Theory*, ed. V. Villanueva, 297–306. Urbana, IL: NCTE.

———. 1992. *Academic Discourse and Critical Consciousness*. Pittsburgh and London: University of Pittsburgh Press.

Braddock, R. 1974. "The Frequency and Placement of Topic Sentences in Expository Prose." *Research in the Teaching of English* 8 (3) (Winter): 287–302. In *Cross-Talk in Comp Theory*, ed. V. Villanueva, 167–81. Urbana, IL: NCTE.

Brannon, L., & G. Pradl. 1984. "The Socialization of Writing Teachers." *The Journal of Basic Writing* 3(4) (Spring/Summer): 28–37.

Britton, J., T. Burgess, N. Martin, A. McLeod, & H. Rosen. 1975. *The Development of Writing Abilities*, 11–18. London: Macmillan Education.

Brodkey, L. 1987. "Modernism and the Scene(s) of Writing." *College English* 49 (4) (April): 396–418.

Brown, C. 1987. "Literacy in 30 Hours: Paulo Freire's Process in Northeast Brazil." In *Freire for the Classroom*, ed. I. Shor, 215–31. Portsmouth, NH: Boynton/Cook.

Brueggemann, B. J. 1999. *Lend Me Your Ear: Rhetorical Constructions of Deafness*. Washington, DC: Gallaudet University Press.

Bruffee, K. A. 1984. "Collaborative Learning and the 'Conversation of Mankind.'" *College English* 46 (7) (November): 635–52. In *Cross-Talk in Comp Theory*, ed. V. Villanueva, 393–414. Urbana, IL: NCTE.

Bruner, M., & M. Oelschlaeger. 1994. "Rhetoric, Environmentalism, and Environmental Ethics." In *Landmark Essays on Rhetoric and the Environment*, ed. C. Waddell, 209–25. Mahwah, NJ: Lawrence Erlbaum Associates.

Buffington, N., M. Diogenes, & C. Moneyhun. 1997. *Living Languages: Contexts for Reading and Writing*. Upper Saddle River, NJ: Prentice Hall.

Charney, D. 1996. "Empiricism Is Not a Four-Letter Word." *College Composition and Communication* 47 (4): 567–93.

Checkley, K. 1997. "The First Seven . . . and the Eighth: A Conversation with Howard Gardner." *Educational Leadership* 55 (1) (September): 8–13.

Childers, P. 1999. "Applying the Ninth Intelligence." Paper presented at Fourth National Writing Across the Curriculum Conference. Cornell University, Ithaca, New York, June 5.

Childers, P. B., E. H. Hobson, & Joan A. Mullin. 1998. *ARTiculating: Teaching Writing in a Visual World*. Portsmouth, NH: Boynton/Cook.

Colloton, A. 2000. Personal interview. May 1. Normal, IL.

Crowley, S. 1995. "Biting the Hand That Feeds Us: Nineteenth Century Uses of a Pedagogy of Taste." In *Rhetoric, Cultural Studies, and Literacy* (Selected Papers from the 1994 Conference of the Rhetoric Society of America), ed. J. F. Reynolds, 11–20. Mahwah, NJ: Lawrence Erlbaum Associates.

———. 1998. *Composition in the University: Historical and Polemical Essays.* Pittsburgh: University of Pittsburgh Press.

Crowley, S., & D. Hawhee. [1994] 1999. *Ancient Rhetorics for Contemporary Students.* 2d ed. Boston: Allyn and Bacon.

Daiker, D. 1989. "Learning to Praise." In *Writing and Response,* ed. C. M. Anson, 103–13. Urbana, IL: NCTE.

Damasio, A. 1999. *The Feeling of What Happens: Body and Emotion in the Making of Consciousness.* New York: Harcourt Brace and Company.

Daniell, B. 1999. "Narratives of Literacy: Connecting Composition to Culture." *College Composition and Communication* 50 (3) (February): 393–410.

Delpit, L. 1988. "The Silenced Dialogue." *Harvard Educational Review* 58 (3) (August): 280–98. In *Cross-Talk in Comp Theory,* ed. V. Villanueva, 565–88. Urbana, IL: NCTE.

Dickinson, E. [1890] 1961. *Final Harvest: Emily Dickinson's Poems.* Selection and Introduction by Thomas H. Johnson. Boston and Toronto: Little, Brown.

Diederich, P. 1974. *Measuring Growth in English.* Urbana, IL: NCTE.

"Dumb and Dumber? An Invitation to a Dialogue on America's Intellectual Capacity." 2000. (Editorial) *U.S. News & World Report.* March 20, 2000, page 20.

Dunn, P. A. 1995. *Learning Re-Abled: The Learning Disability Controversy and Composition Studies.* Portsmouth, NH: Boynton/Cook.

Dunn, R., & K. Dunn. 1993. *Teaching Secondary Students Through Their Individual Learning Styles: Practical Approaches for Grades 7–12.* Boston: Allyn and Bacon.

Elbow, P. 1973. *Writing Without Teachers.* New York: Oxford University Press.

———. 1985. "The Shifting Relationships Between Speech and Writing." *College Composition and Communication* 36(3)6 (October): 283–303.

———. 1986. *Embracing Contraries: Explorations in Learning and Teaching.* New York: Oxford University Press.

———. 1993. "Ranking, Evaluating, and Liking: Sorting Out Three Forms of Judgment." *College English* 55 (2) (February): 187–206.

Elias, J. L. 1994. *Paulo Freire: Pedagogue of Liberation.* Malabar, FL: Kreiger Publishing Company.

Emig, J. 1977. "Writing as a Mode of Learning." *College Composition and Communication* 28 (2) (May): 120–28. In *Cross-Talk in Comp Theory,* ed. V. Villanueva, 7–15. Urbana, IL: NCTE.

———. 1978. "Hand, Eye, Brain: Some 'Basics' in the Writing Process." In *Research on Composing: Points of Departure*, eds. C. R. Cooper and L. Odell, 59–71. Urbana, IL: NCTE.

———. 1997. "Writing as a Mode of Learning." In *Cross-Talk in Comp Theory*, ed.V. Villanueva. Urbana, IL: NCTE.

Eriksson, S. 1999. "Metaphors in Teaching Geology—More Than a 'Literary Frill'" Paper presented at Fourth National Writing Across the Curriculum Conference. Cornell University, Ithaca, New York, June 4.

Fahnestock, J., & M. Secor. 1991. "The Rhetoric of Literary Criticism." In *Textual Dynamics of the Profession: Historical and Contemporary Studies of Writing in the Professions*, eds. C. Bazerman and J. Paradis, 76–96. Madison: The University of Wisconsin Press.

Faigley, L. [1992] 1995. *Fragments of Rationality: Postmodernity and the Subject of Composition*. Pittsburgh and London: University of Pittsburgh Press.

Farris, C., & C. M. Anson. 1998. *Under Construction: Working at the Intersections of Composition Theory, Research, and Practice*. Logan, UT: Utah University Press.

Finlay, L. S., & V. Faith. 1979. "Illiteracy and Alienation in American Colleges: Is Paulo Freire's Pedagogy Relevant?" *Radical Teacher* 16: 28–37. In *Freire for the Classroom*, ed. I. Shor, 63–86. Portsmouth, NH: Boynton/Cook.

Fiore, K., & N. Elasser. 1982. "'Strangers No More': A Liberatory Literacy Curriculum." *College English* 44 (2) (February): 115–28. In *Freire for the Classroom*, ed. I. Shor, 87–103. Portsmouth: NH: Boynton/Cook.

Flynn, E. A., K. Remlinger, & W. Bulleit. 1997. "Interaction Across the Curriculum." *JAC* 17 (3): 343–64.

Forman, E. A., & C. B. Cazden. [1985] 1989. "Exploring Vygotskian Perspectives in Education: The Cognitive Value of Peer Interaction." In *Culture, Communication, and Cognition: Vygotskian Perspectives*, ed. J. V. Wertsch, 323–47. Cambridge: Cambridge University Press.

Fox, T. 1999. *Defending Access: A Critique of Standards in Higher Education*. Portsmouth, NH: Boynton/Cook.

Freire, P. [1968] 1973. *The Pedagogy of the Oppressed*. Translation by Myra Bergman Ramos. NY: The Seabury Press—A Continuum Book.

———. 1973. "By Learning They Can Teach." *Convergence* 6 (1): 78–84.

———. 1993. *Education for Critical Consciousness*. New York: Continuum.

Freire, P., & D. Macedo. 1987. *Literacy: Reading the Word and the World*. South Hadley, MA: Bergin & Garvey.

Freire, P., ed., with J. W. Fraser, D. Macedo, T. McKinnon, & W. T. Stokes. 1997. *Mentoring the Mentor: A Critical Dialogue with Paulo Freire*. New York: Peter Lang Publishing.

Fulkerson, J., & M. Horvich. 1998. "Talent Development: Two Perspectives." *Phi Delta Kappan* (June): 756–59.

Gage, R. 1995. "Excuse Me, You're Cramping My Style: Kinesthetics for the Classroom." *English Journal* 84 (8) (December): 52–55.

Gardner, H. [1983] 1985. *Frames of Mind: The Theory of Multiple Intelligences.* New York: Basic Books.

———. 1995. "'Multiple Intelligences' as a Catalyst." *English Journal* 84 (8) (December): 16–18.

Gilyard, K. 1996a. "An African American in Process." In *Let's Flip the Script: An African American Discourse on Language, Literature, and Learning,* 87–96. Detroit: Wayne State University Press.

———. 1996b. "One More Time for Professor Nuruddin." In *Let's Flip the Script: An African American Discourse on Language, Literature, and Learning,* 63–71. Detroit: Wayne State University Press.

Giroux, H. A. 1993. "Paulo Freire and the Politics of Post-Colonialism." In *Paulo Freire: A Critical Encounter,* eds. P. McLaren & P. Leonard. London and New York: Routledge.

———. 1997. "Remembering Paulo Freire." *JAC* 17 (3): 310–13.

Glasgow, J. N., & M. S. Bush. 1995. "Promoting Active Learning and Collaborative Writing Through a Marketing Project." *English Journal* 84 (8) (December): 32–37.

Goleman, D. 1995. *Emotional Intelligence.* New York: Bantam Books.

Graff, G. 1997. "Other Voices, Other Rooms." In *Living Languages,* eds. N. Buffington, M. Diogenes, & C. Moneyhon, 150–55. (An excerpt from *Beyond the Culture Wars,* 1992.)

Gross, A. 1999. "Toward More Perfect Union: Bridging the Gap Between the Sciences and the Humanities." Paper presented at Fourth National Writing Across the Curriculum Conference. Cornell University, Ithaca, New York, June 4.

Guskin, S. L., C. J. Peng, & M. Simon. 1992. "Do Teachers React to 'Multiple Intelligences'? Effects of Teachers' Stereotypes on Judgements and Expectations for Students with Diverse Patterns of Giftedness/Talent." *Gifted Child Quarterly* 36 (1) (Winter): 32–37.

Halloran, S. M. 1984. "The Birth of Molecular Biology: An Essay in the Rhetorical Criticism of Scientific Discourse." *Rhetoric Review* 3: 70–83. In *Landmark Essays on Rhetoric of Science,* ed. R. A. Harris, 39–50.

Halloran, S. M., & A. N. Bradford. 1984. "Figures of Speech in the Rhetoric of Science and Technology." In *Essays on Classical Rhetoric and Modern Discourse,* eds. R. J. Connors, L. S. Ede, & A. Lunsford, 179–92. Carbondale and Edwardsville: Southern Illinois University Press.

Harrison, S. 2000. "Cyborgs and Digital Sound Writing: Rearticulating Automated Speech Recognition Typing Programs." Online journal. *Kairos* 5 (1) <http://english.ttu.edu/kairos/5.1/features/harrison/cybwrt5.html>.

Hartwell, P. 1985. "Grammar, Grammars, and the Teaching of Grammar." *College English* 47 (2): 105–27.

Hecker, L. 1997. "Walking, Tinkertoys, and Legos: Using Movement and Manipulatives to Help Students Write." *English Journal* 86 (6) (October): 46–52.

Hobson, E. 1999. "The Argument for a Ninth Intelligence." Paper presented at Fourth National Writing Across the Curriculum Conference. Cornell University, Ithaca, New York, June 5.

hooks, b. 1989. *Talking Back*. Boston: South End Press.

———. 1994. *Teaching to Transgress: Education as the Practice of Freedom*. New York and London: Routledge.

Howard, R. M. 1999. *Standing in the Shadow of Giants: Plagiarists, Authors, Collaborators*. Stamford, CT: Ablex.

Hurston, Z. N. [1933] 1995. "The Gilded Six Bits." In *Zora Neale Hurston: The Complete Stories*, introduction by H. L. Gates, Jr., & S. Lemke, 86–98. New York: Harper Perrennial. ("The Gilded Six Bits" was originally published in *Story*, August 1933.)

Jung, J. 1997. "Revision Hope: Writing Disruption in Composition Studies." *JAC* 17 (3): 427–52.

Kelman, M., & G. Lester. 1998. *Jumping the Queue: An Inquiry into the Legal Treatment of Students with Learning Disabilities*. Cambridge, MA: Harvard University Press.

Kirby, D., & T. Liner, with R. Vinz. [1988] 1991. *Inside Out: Developmental Strategies for Teaching Writing*. 2d ed. Portsmouth, NH: Boynton/Cook.

Klein, K., & L. Hecker. 1994. "The Write Moves: Cultivating Kinesthetic and Spatial Intelligences in the Writing Process." In *Presence of Mind: Writing Beyond the Cognitive Domain*, eds. A. Brand & R. Graves, 89–98. Portsmouth, NH: Heinemann.

Knoblauch, C. H. 1988. "Rhetorical Constructions: Dialogue and Commitment." *College English* 50(2): 125–40.

Knoblauch, C. H., & L. Brannon. 1981. "Teacher Commentary on Student Writing: The State of the Art." *Freshman English News* 10 (2) (fall): 1–4.

———. 1984. *Rhetorical Traditions and the Teaching of Writing*. Upper Montclair, NJ: Boynton/Cook.

Kutz, E., & H. Roskelly. 1991. *An Unquiet Pedagogy: Transforming Practice in the English Classroom*. Portsmouth, NH: Boynton/Cook.

Labov, W. 1966. *The Social Stratification of English in New York City*. Washington, DC: Center for Applied Linguistics.

Lakoff, G., & M. Johnson. 1980. *Metaphors We Live By*. Chicago and London: The University of Chicago Press.

Laird, C. 1970. *Language in America*. New York: World.

Larson, R. L. 1982. "The 'Research Paper' in the Writing Course: A Non-Form of Writing." *College English* 44 (8) (December): 811–16.

LeCourt, D. 1996. "WAC as Critical Pedagogy: The Third Stage?" *JAC* 16 (3): 389–405.

Lightfoot, M., & N. Martin. 1988. *The Word for Teaching is Learning. Language and Learning Today Essays for James Britton*, in association with National Association for the Teaching of English. London: Heinemann Educational Books and Portsmouth, NH: Boynton/Cook.

Lowe, C. 2000. "Continuous Speech Recognition: Not Just a New Technology." Paper presented at CCCC, Minneapolis, April 14.

Lyman, D. E. 1986. *Making the Words Stand Still.* Boston: Houghton Mifflin.

Mahala, D. 1991. "Writing Utopias: Writing Across the Curriculum and the Promise of Reform." *College English* 53 (7): 773–89.

Martin, N. 1976. "Language Across the Curriculum: A Paradox and Its Potential for Change." *Educational Review* 28: 206–19.

Mayher, J. S. 1990. *Uncommon Sense: Theoretical Practice in Language Education.* Portsmouth, NH: Boynton/Cook.

McKeon, R. 1987. *Rhetoric: Essays in Invention and Discovery.* Woodbridge, CT: Ox Bow Press.

McLaren, P., & P. Leonard. 1993. *Paulo Freire: A Critical Encounter.* London and New York: Routledge.

Metcalf, S. D. 1998. "Attention Deficits: Does Special Education Leave Many Poor Learners Behind?" *Lingua Franca* (March): 60–65.

Miller, R. E. 1998. "The Arts of Complicity: Pragmatism and the Culture of Schooling." *College English* 61 (1) (September): 10–28.

Minock, M. 1996. "A(n) (Un)Certain Synergy: Rhetoric, Hermaneutics, and Transdisciplinary Conversations About Writing." *College Composition and Communication* 47 (4) (December): 502–22.

Moffett, J. 1981. *Active Voice: A Writing Program Across the Curriculum.* Montclair, NJ: Boynton/Cook.

Mullin, J. 1999. "Seeing as Teaching: A Study of Visuals Across the Disciplines." Paper presented at Fourth National Writing Across the Curriculum Conference. Cornell University, Ithaca, New York, June 5.

Myers, G. 1986. "Reality, Consensus and Reform in the Rhetoric of Composition Teaching" *College English* 48 (2) (February): 154–74. In *Cross-Talk in Comp Theory,* ed, V. Villanueva, Jr., 415–37. Urbana, IL: NCTE.

North, S. M. 1987. *The Making of Knowledge in Composition: Portrait of an Emerging Field.* Upper Montclair, NJ: Boynton/Cook.

North, S. M., with B. A. Chepaitis, D. Coogan, L. Davidson, R. MacLean, C. L. Parrish, J. Post, & B. Weatherby. 2000. *Refiguring the Ph.D. in English Studies: Writing, Doctoral Education, and the Fusion-Based Curriculum.* Urbana, IL: NCTE.

Null, R. L., with K. F. Cherry. 1998. *Universal Design: Creative Solutions for ADA Compliance.* Belmont, CA: Professional Publications.

Oakeshott, M. 1962. *Rationalism in Politics.* New York: Basic Books.

Ohmann, R. 1979. "Use Definite, Specific, Concrete Language." *College English* 41 (4) (December): 390–97.

Ong, W. J. 1982, 1987. *Orality and Literacy: The Technologizing of the Word.* London and New York: Methuen.

Onore, C. 1989. "The Student, the Teacher, and the Text: Negotiating Meanings Through Response and Revision." In *Writing and Response: Theory, Practice, and Research,* ed. C. M. Anson, 231–60. Urbana, IL: NCTE.

Osburg, B. 1995. "Multiple Intelligences: A New Category of Losers." *English Journal* 84 (8) (December): 13–15.

Parker, K. 2000. "Legos Test: Wrong Way to Decide Who Goes to College." *The Pantagraph.* Feb 14, 2000. A8. (Syndicated by Media Services through *The Chicago Tribune.*)

Parker, R. P. 1982. "Language, Schools, and the Growth of Mind." *CEA Critic* 43 (January): 6–13.

———. 1985. "The 'Language Across the Curriculum' Movement: A Brief Overview and Bibliography." *College Composition and Communication* 36 (2) (May): 173–77.

Parker, R. P., & V. Goodkin. 1987. *The Consequences of Writing: Enhancing Learning in the Disciplines.* Upper Montclair, NJ: Boynton/Cook.

Perelman, C., & L. Olbrechts-Tyteca. 1969. *The New Rhetoric: A Treatise on Argument.* Notre Dame: University of Notre Dame Press.

Phelps, L. W. 1988. *Composition as a Human Science: Contributions to the Self-Understanding of a Discipline.* New York: Oxford University Press.

Pierpoint, A. 1996. Letter to the Editor. *English Journal* 85 (2) (February): 11–12.

Pirie, B. 1995. "Meaning Through Motion: Kinesthetic English." *English Journal* 84 (8) (December): 46–51.

Ponsot, M., & R. Deen. 1982. *Beat Not the Poor Desk.* Upper Montclair, NJ: Boynton/Cook.

Porter, J. E. 1986. "Intertextuality and the Discourse Community." *Rhetoric Review* 5 (1): 34–47.

Porter, J. E., P. Sullivan, S. Blythe, J. T. Grabill, & L. Miles. 2000. "Institutional Critique: A Rhetorical Methodology for Change." *College Composition and Communication* 51 (4) (June): 610–42.

Ray, R., & E. Barton. 1998. "Farther Afield: Rethinking the Contributions of Research." In *Under Construction: Working at the Intersections of Composition Theory, Research, and Practice,* eds. C. Farris & C. M. Anson, 196–214. Logan, UT: Utah State University Press.

Reece, J. E., & G. Cumming. 1996. "Evaluating Speech-Based Composition Methods: Planning, Dictation, and the Listening Word Processor" In *The Science of Writing: Theories, Methods, Individual Differences, and Applications,* eds. C. M. Levy & S. Ransdell, 361–80. Mahwah, NJ: Lawrence Erlbaum Associates.

Reid, C., & B. Romanoff. 1997. "Using Multiple Intelligence Theory to Identify Gifted Children." *Educational Leadership* 55 (1) (September): 71–74.

Rodriguez, R. 1982. *Hunger of Memory.* Boston: D. R. Godine.

———. 1997. "Aria: A Memoir of a Bilingual Childhood." In *Living Languages: Contexts for Reading and Writing,* eds. N. Buffington, M. Diogenes, & C. Moneyhun, 98–109. Upper Saddle River, NJ: Prentice Hall.

Ronald, K., & H. Roskelly. 1990. *Farther Along: Transforming Dichotomies in Rhetoric and Composition*. Portsmouth, NH: Boynton/Cook.

Rorty, R. 1979. *Philosophy and the Mirror of Nature*. Princeton, NJ: Princeton University Press.

———. 1991. *Objectivity, Relativism, and Truth: Philosophical Papers*. Cambridge and New York: Cambridge University Press.

Rose, M. 1988. "Narrowing the Mind and the Page: Remedial Writers and Cognitive Reductionism." *College Composition and Communication* 39 (3) (October): 267–98. In *Cross-Talk in Comp Theory*, ed. V. Villanueva, 323–63. Urbana, IL: NCTE.

———.1989. *Lives on the Boundary*. New York: Simon & Schuster.

Royster, J. J. 1999. "Sarah's Story: Making a Place for Historical Ethnography in Rhetorical Studies." In *Rhetoric, the Polis, and the Global Village* (Selected Papers from the 1998 Thirtieth Anniversary Rhetoric Society of America Conference), 39–51. Mahwah, NJ: Lawrence Erlbaum Associates.

Russell, D. R. 1991. *Writing in the Academic Disciplines, 1870–1990: A Curricular History*. Carbondale: Southern Illinois University Press.

Sacks, O. 1995. *An Anthropologist on Mars*. New York: Vintage Books.

Schaff, A. 1973. *Language and Cognition*. New York: McGraw-Hill.

Schell, E. E. 1998. *Gypsy Academics and Mother-Teachers: Gender, Contingent Labor, and Writing Instruction*. Portsmouth, NH: Boynton/Cook.

Scholes, R. 1985. *Textual Power: Literary Theory and the Teaching of English*. New Haven and London: Yale University Press.

Schuster, C. I. 1985. "Mikhail Bakhtin as Rhetorical Theorist." *College English* 47 (6) (October): 594–607. In *Cross-Talk in Comp Theory*, ed. V. Villanueva, 457–73. Urbana, IL: NCTE.

Selfe, C. L. 1999. "Technology and Literacy: A Story About the Perils of Not Paying Attention." *College Composition and Communication* 50 (3) (February): 411–36.

Shaughnessy, M. P. 1976. "Diving In: An Introduction to Basic Writing." *College Composition and Communication* 27 (3) (October): 234–39.

———. 1977. *Errors and Expectations: A Guide for the Teacher of Basic Writing*. New York: Oxford University Press.

Shor, I. 1980. *Critical Teaching and Everyday Life*. Boston: South End Press.

———. 1987. *Freire for the Classroom: A Sourcebook for Liberatory Teaching*. Portsmouth, NH: Boynton/Cook.

———. 1993. "Education Is Politics: Paulo Freire's Critical Pedagogy." In *Paulo Freire: A Critical Encounter*, eds. P. McLaren & P. Leonard, 25–35. London and New York: Routledge.

Shor, I., & C. Pari. 1999. *Education Is Politics: Critical Teaching Across Differences K–12*. Portsmouth, NH: Boynton/Cook.

Simeone, W. F. 1995. "Accommodating Multiple Intelligences in the English Classroom." *English Journal* 84 (8) (December): 60–62.

Smagorinsky, P. 1991. *Expressions: Multiple Intelligences in the English Class*. Urbana, IL: NCTE.

———. 1995. "Multiple Intelligences in the English Class: An Overview." *English Journal* 84 (8) (December): 19–26.

Smitherman, G. 1999. "CCCC's Role in the Struggle for Language Rights." *College Composition and Communication* 50 (3) (February): 349–76.

Sommers, N. 1980. "Revision Strategies of Student Writers and Experienced Adult Writers." *College Composition and Communication* 31 (4) (December): 378–88. In *Cross-Talk in Comp Theory*, ed. V. Villanueva. Urbana, IL: NCTE.

Soper, K. 2000. "Things You Shouldn't Say at Your Dissertation Defense" (Cartoon). *The Chronicle of Higher Education* (July 7): B11.

Taylor, P. V. 1993. *The Texts of Paulo Freire*. Buckingham and Philadelphia: Open University Press.

Thomas, C. 2000. "School Choice: No Place Like Home for Right Education." *The Pantagraph* (June 7): A13. (Distributed by *Los Angeles Times* Syndicate.)

Thomas, D., & G. Thomas. 1989. "The Use of Rogerian Reflection in Small-Group Writing Conferences." In *Writing and Response: Theory, Practice, and Research*, ed. C. M. Anson, 114–26. Urbana, IL: NCTE.

Tompkins, J. 1985. "Sentimental Power: *Uncle Tom's Cabin* and the Politics of Literary History." In *Sensational Designs: The Cultural Work of American Fiction*, 122–46. New York: Oxford University Press.

Torres, R.-M. 1998. "The Million Paulo Freires." *Convergence* tribute to Paulo Freire 31 (1 & 2): 107–16.

Trimbur, J. 1989. "Consensus and Difference in Collaborative Learning." *College English* 51 (6): 602–16. In *Cross-Talk in Comp Theory*, ed. V. Villanueva, 439–55. Urbana, IL: NCTE.

Tucker, B. 1995. "Minds of Their Own: Visualizers Compose." *English Journal* 84 (8) (December): 27–31.

Twain, M. 1983. "The War Prayer." In *Mark Twain: Selected Writings of an American Skeptic*, ed. Victor Doyno, 423–25. Buffalo, NY: Prometheus Books.

Villanueva, V., Jr. 1987. "Whose Voice Is It Anyway? Rodriguez' Speech in Retrospect." *English Journal* 76 (8) (December): 17–21.

———. 1997. *Cross-Talk in Comp Theory: A Reader*. Urbana, IL: NCTE.

Vygotsky, L. S. 1978. *Mind in Society: The Development of Higher Psychological Processes*. Eds. V. John-Steiner, M. Cole, E. Souberman, & S. Scribner. Cambridge and London: Harvard University Press.

———. [1986] 1989. *Thought and Language*. Ed. A. Kozulin. Cambridge and London: The MIT Press.

Waldron, A. 2000. "Where Writing Happens: The Use of Venn Diagrams in Understanding Argument." Paper presented at CCCC 2000, Minneapolis, April 13.

Wallerstein, N., & E. Bernstein. 1999. "Empowerment Education: Freire's Ideas Adapted to Health Education." In *Education is Politics*, eds. I. Shor and C. Pari, 53–71. Portsmouth, NH: Boynton/Cook.

Washington, G. 1996. "The Writing Crisis in Urban Schools: A Culturally Different Hypothesis." *JAC* 16.3: 425–33.

Wertsch, J. V. 1985, 1989. *Culture, Communication, and Cognition: Vygotskian Perspectives.* Cambridge: Cambridge University Press.

West, T. 1991, 1997. *In the Mind's Eye: Visual Thinkers, Gifted People with Dyslexia and Other Learning Difficulties, Computer Images and the Ironies of Creativity.* New York: Prometheus Books.

Wiley, M., B. Gleason, & L. W. Phelps. 1996. *Composition in Four Keys: Inquiring into the Field.* Mountain View, CA: Mayfield.

Williams, J. M. 1981. "The Phenomenology of Error." *College Composition and Communication* 32 (2) (March): 152–68.

Witte, S. P., & L. Faigley. 1981. "Coherence, Cohesion, and Writing Quality." *College Composition and Communication* 32 (2) (May): 189–204.

Zebroski, J. T. 1994. *Thinking Through Theory: Vygotskian Perspectives on the Teaching of Writing.* Portsmouth, NH: Boynton/Cook.

———. 1998. "Toward a Theory of Theory for Composition Studies." In *Under Construction: Working at the Intersections of Composition Theory, Research, and Practice,* eds. C. Farris & C. M. Anson, 30–48. Logan, UT: Utah State University Press.

Zemelman, S., & H. Daniels. 1993. "Defining the Process Paradigm." In *Linguistics for Teachers,* eds. L. M. Cleary and M. D. Linn, 339–56. New York: McGraw-Hill.

Index